THOMAS AQUINAS

Treatise on Law

(*Summa Theologica,* Questions 90-97)

With an Introduction

by Stanley Parry

A Gateway Edition
Regnery Gateway
Washington, D.C.

Photo courtesy of John M. Wing Foundation
The Newberry Library, Chicago. *The Judgement of Solomon*
Text reprinted from the *Summa Theologica*
with the permission of Benziger Brothers, Inc.
Publishers and copyright owners.

Published in the United States by
Regnery Gateway, Inc.
1130 17th St., N.W.
Washington, D.C. 20036

Distributed to the trade by
National Book Network
4720-A Boston Way
Lanham, MD 20706

Manufactured in the United States of America
1991 printing
Printed on acid-free paper

International Standard Book Number: 0-89526-918-X

CONTENTS

Aquinas' Philosophy of Law

IN THE *Treatise on Law*, Aquinas offers a philo-
sophical analysis of the structure of law. The deeper
significance of this analysis lies in its struggle with
the problem of moral obligation in the political order,
a problem which Aquinas approaches with an observation of fact and an interpretation of that fact. The
observation of fact is that men in society live under
law; the interpretation of the fact is that law
achieves its results by imposing moral obligation
rather than outright force on those subject to it.
Out of such an interpretation the problem arises:
what is the source of this obligation? Aquinas does
not ask *why* men live under law, nor is he formally
concerned with proving that law imposes moral obligation. His concern focuses almost exclusively on
one problem, that of the roots of obligation. The
problem is basic because it asks, in effect, by what
warrant the human legislator binds the consciences
of men. Is not this a power that belongs to God alone?
If men possess it, what are the limits within which
they may exercise it?

The answer Aquinas gives to these questions is a
simple one: "Laws framed by men are either just or

unjust. If they be just, they have the power of binding in conscience, from the eternal law whence they
are derived. . . ." (Quest. 96, art. 4). The thought
leading to this conclusion, though complex in its full
expression, advances through three simple and basic
propositions: (1) obligation is a property that inheres
in the nature of things (Quest. 95, art. 2), (2) since
man has no control over the nature of things, he has
no power to determine the basic outlines of obligation (Quest. 93, art. 5), and (3) since the nature
of finite things is not self-explanatory, the ultimate
source of obligation must be found in the infinite
Being who does determine the nature of things
(Quest. 93, art. 4). Thus the source of obligation is
in the divine conception of the order proper to the
universe. As Aquinas concludes: ". . . the plan of
government is derived by secondary governors from
the governor in chief. . . . Since then the eternal law
is the plan of government in the Chief Governor, all
the plans of government in the inferior governors
must be derived from the eternal law" (Quest. 93,
art. 3).

Even this brief outline of his answer distinguishes
Aquinas from those whose theories are based on the
Hobbesian hypothesis that human will, whether individual or corporate, can originate law. The great
truth stressed is that law, insofar as it is morally
obligating, must be rooted in God. Although there
is a human authority residing in the people by force
of nature (Quest. 90, art. 3), not even the people
are the original possessors of this power to impose

obligation. Aquinas rejects the Divine Right theory
because it explains the power of law to bind conscience by attributing a divine quality to political
authority. No political authority, not even the sovereign authority, can impose an obligation on the
citizen where it is not already latent in the nature of
things.

Granted that human law must conform to eternal
law, the human legislator still must have some way
of discovering what the directives of eternal law are.
The Romanticist solves the problem by his direct acceptance of primitive nature. But this acceptance
rests on an emotional or instinctive basis which
Aquinas cannot admit. His own solution is an intel-
lectualist one which begins with the premise: "Now
the rule and measure of human acts is the reason,
which is the first principal of human acts. . . . Consequently it follows that law is something pertaining
to reason" (Quest. 90, art. 1). Therefore, just as
human law does not impose obligation until it is
known to the subject, so also eternal law cannot
guide the human legislator until its directives are
made evident to him in some way. The use of the
terms "right reason" and "natural law," which is
sometimes confusing to the reader, becomes clear
when one keeps in mind that man must know the
law of nature before it can become a guide to action.
Obligation lies in the nature of things, but it orig-
inates in the mind of God and terminates in the
mind of man. Natural law is the objective link between the mind of man and the mind of God. Right

eternal law through its understanding of the moral reason is human reason acting in harmony with imperatives inherent in the nature of things.

By creation God sets finite beings in existence apart from Himself. Each of these beings has a nature. Natures or natural things, as Aristotle defines them, are those things which "have within [themselves] a principle of motion and of stationariness." Now for our purposes, the most relevant aspect of this principle has to do with growth. In the case of man, growth is achieved most obviously in the physical order. But man "grows" in other ways: his intellect develops, his will stabilizes on morally good objects. Such growth, however, is not automatic as in the physical order, but the result of a consciously organized plan of action. The general outlines of this plan of action are pre-determined by the tendencies of man's nature, just as the growth of man's body is pre-determined by tendencies inherent in the physical parts of his nature. Man must therefore read nature in order to discover the type of action by which human nature is perfected. Since eternal law is promulgated in the natural order by the very creation of natures, it follows that natural law is not something different from eternal law but rather a "participation thereof" (Quest. 91, art. 2) which the human legislator must study to discover the mind of God (Quest. 92, art. 2 and 3).

This idea of the way eternal law is promulgated is fundamental to Aquinas's theory of how obligation is transmitted from God to human legislator to citizen.

It keeps before our minds that the issue is not the transfer of a right to rule but the source of the authority which a rightful ruler exercises.

Thus, Aquinas' explanation of the origins of obligation depends on his conception of natural law. It is through the mind's ability to recognize the imperatives of nature that God communicates to man the basic patterns of action proper to him. Moreover, in this process man does not play the part of an automaton. He does not dangle at the end of cosmic puppet strings. Both eternal and natural law are generalized patterns of action, and man, therefore, in determining action in the concrete circumstances of life, contributes something to the determination of right action. The three laws—eternal, natural and human—are not three independent rules of action but one rule progressively specified (Quest. 95, art. 2).

With regard to such political problems as the form of government and the wisdom of particular public policies, the *Treatise* has nothing to say. Basic to it, however, is an implied position on the relationship between law and freedom which, if accepted, will profoundly influence one's conception of the problem of politics. In the Thomistic philosophy of law, human liberty is not an absolute condition. Man exists in the midst of realities which he must recognize and respect if he is to live a human life. He is inherently limited, both morally and physically, by laws that determine the total order of which he is a part. Freedom, or free will, consequently, is the faculty of judging for oneself the demands of reality. As Laversin says: "The autonomy of the individual will can be understood only as an abstraction, that is to say, only by considering man's power to act as existing independently of his being and the conditions of actual existence." Law, insofar as it puts into concrete terms the general imperatives of nature, is not an adventitious limiting of action. Rather it is a conscious recognition and corporate specification of the natural boundaries of action in the real conditions of life. Thus law is perfectly compatible with the freedom proper to man.

This is not to deny that problems arise with regard to the government that makes the law. For it does not follow from this harmony between law and freedom that a just law cannot also be oppressive. But it does mean that a political philosophy based on the premise of harmony will be radically different from philosophies that begin with a premise of conflict. Utilitarian thought, for instance, begins with the premise that action under law is not free. Behind this premise is the idea that spontaneity is the essential element in freedom. Law, by imposing a rule of action on the citizen in the name of the group, destroys this element of spontaneity and so freedom.

From these two positions there follow two different conceptions of the problem of politics. The problem for the Thomist is to work out a system of government that will realize in fact the theoretical harmony between law and freedom. The problem for the Utilitarian is to work out a system that will sacrifice as little freedom as is compatible with the preservation of order. The one philosophy supports the theory that all men can conceivably achieve complete freedom; the other begins by supposing that a sacrifice of freedom is inevitable.

STANLEY PARRY

University of Notre Dame

OF THE ESSENCE OF LAW

(In Four Articles)

WE have now to consider the extrinsic principles of acts. Now the extrinsic principle inclining to evil is the devil, of whose temptations we have spoken in the First Part (Q. CXIV.). But the extrinsic principle moving to good is God, Who both instructs us by means of His Law, and assists us by His Grace: wherefore in the first place we must speak of law; in the second place, of grace.

Concerning law, we must consider—(1) Law itself in general; (2) Its parts. Concerning law in general three points offer themselves for our consideration: (1) Its essence; (2) The different kinds of law; (3) The effects of law.

Under the first head there are four points of inquiry: (1) Whether law is something pertaining to reason? (2) Concerning the end of law. (3) Its cause. (4) The promulgation of law.

First Article

WHETHER LAW IS SOMETHING PERTAINING TO REASON

We proceed thus to the First Article:—

Objection 1. It would seem that law is not something pertaining to reason. For the Apostle says (Rom. vii. 23): *I see another law in my members,* etc. But nothing pertaining to reason is in the members; since the reason does not make use of a bodily organ. Therefore law is not something pertaining to reason.

Obj. 2. Further, in the reason there is nothing else but power, habit, and act. But law is not the power itself of reason. In like manner, neither is it a habit of reason: because the habits of reason are the intellectual virtues of which we have spoken above (Q. LVII.). Nor again is it an act of reason: because then law would cease, when the act of reason ceases, for instance, while we are asleep. Therefore law is nothing pertaining to reason.

Obj. 3. Further, the law moves those who are subject to it to act aright. But it belongs properly to the will to move to act, as is evident from what has been said above (Q. IX., A. 1). Therefore law pertains, not to the reason, but to the will; according to the words of the Jurist (*Lib.* i. *ff., De Const. Prin.* leg. i.): *Whatsoever pleaseth the sovereign, has force of law.*

On the contrary, It belongs to the law to command and to forbid. But it belongs to reason to command, as stated above (Q. XVII., A. 1). Therefore law is something pertaining to reason.

I answer that, Law is a rule and measure of acts, whereby man is induced to act or is restrained from acting: for *lex* (law) is derived from *ligare* (to bind), because it binds one to act. Now the rule and measure of human acts is the reason, which is the first principle of human acts, as is evident from what has been stated above (Q. I., A. 1 *ad* 3); since it belongs to the reason to direct to the end, which is the first principle in all matters of action, according to the Philosopher (*Phys.* ii.). Now that which is the principle in any genus, is the rule and measure of that genus: for instance, unity in the genus of numbers, and the first movement in the genus of movements. Consequently it follows that law is something pertaining to reason.

Reply Obj. 1. Since law is a kind of rule and measure, it may be in something in two ways. First, as in that which measures and rules: and since this is proper to reason, it follows that, in this way, law is in the reason alone.—Secondly, as in that which is measured and ruled. In this way, law is in all those things that are inclined to something by reason of some law: so that any inclination arising from a law, may be called a law, not essentially but by participation as it were. And thus the inclination of the members to concupiscence is called *the law of the members.*

Reply Obj. 2. Just as, in external action, we may

consider the work and the work done, for instance
the work of building and the house built; so in the
acts of reason, we may consider the act itself of reason, i.e., to understand and to reason, and something
produced by this act. With regard to the speculative
reason, this is first of all the definition; secondly, the
proposition; thirdly, the syllogism or argument. And
since also the practical reason makes use of a syllogism in respect of the work to be done, as stated above
(Q. XIII., A. 3; Q. LXXVI., A. 1) and as the Philosopher teaches (*Ethic.* vii. 3); hence we find in
the practical reason something that holds the same
position in regard to operations, as, in the speculative
intellect, the proposition holds in regard to conclusions. Suchlike universal propositions of the practical
intellect that are directed to actions have the nature
of law. And these propositions are sometimes under
our actual consideration, while sometimes they are
retained in the reason by means of a habit.

Reply Obj. 3. Reason has its power of moving
from the will, as stated above (Q. XVII., A. 1): for
it is due to the fact that one wills the end, that the
reason issues its commands as regards things ordained
to the end. But in order that the volition of what is
commanded may have the nature of law, it needs to
be in accord with some rule of reason. And in this
sense is to be understood the saying that the will of
the sovereign has the force of law; otherwise the
sovereign's will would savour of lawlessness rather
than of law.

SECOND ARTICLE

WHETHER THE LAW IS ALWAYS DIRECTED TO THE COMMON GOOD?

We proceed thus to the Second Article:—

Objection 1. It would seem that the law is not always directed to the common good as to its end. For it belongs to law to command and to forbid. But commands are directed to certain individual goods. Therefore the end of the law is not always the common good.

Obj. 2. Further, the law directs man in his actions. But human actions are concerned with particular matters. Therefore the law is directed to some particular good.

Obj. 3. Further, Isidore says (*Etym.* v. 3): *If the law is based on reason, whatever is based on reason will be a law.* But reason is the foundation not only of what is ordained to the common good, but also of that which is directed to private good. Therefore the law is not only directed to the good of all, but also to the private good of an individual.

On the contrary, Isidore says (*Etym.* v. 21) that *laws are enacted for no private profit, but for the common benefit of the citizens.*

I answer that, As stated above (A. 1), the law belongs to that which is a principle of human acts, because it is their rule and measure. Now as reason is a principle of human acts, so in reason itself there is something which is the principle in respect of all the rest: wherefore to this principle chiefly and mainly law must needs be referred.—Now the first principle in practical matters, which are the object of the practical reason, is the last end: and the last end of human life is bliss or happiness, as stated above (Q. II., A. 7; Q. III., A. 1). Consequently the law must needs regard principally the relationship to happiness. Moreover, since every part is ordained to the whole, as imperfect to perfect; and since one man is a part of the perfect community, the law must needs regard properly the relationship to universal happiness. Wherefore the Philosopher, in the above definition of legal matters mentions both happiness and the body politic: for he says (*Ethic.* v. 1) that we call those legal matters *just, which are adapted to produce and preserve happiness and its parts for the body politic:* since the state is a perfect community, as he says in *Polit.* i. 1.

Now in every genus, that which belongs to it chiefly is the principle of the others, and the others belong to that genus in subordination to that thing: thus fire, which is chief among hot things, is the cause of heat in mixed bodies, and these are said to be hot in so far as they have a share of fire. Consequently, since the law is chiefly ordained to the common good, any other precept in regard to some individual work, must needs be devoid of the nature of a law, save in so far as it regards the common good. Therefore every law is ordained to the common good.

Reply Obj. 1. A command denotes an application of a law to matters regulated by the law. Now the order to the common good, at which the law aims, is applicable to particular ends. And in this way commands are given even concerning particular matters.

Reply Obj. 2. Actions are indeed concerned with particular matters: but those particular matters are referable to the common good, not as to a common genus or species, but as to a common final cause, according as the common good is said to be the common end.

Reply Obj. 3. Just as nothing stands firm with regard to the speculative reason except that which is traced back to the first indemonstrable principles, so nothing stands firm with regard to the practical reason, unless it be directed to the last end which is the common good: and whatever stands to reason in this sense, has the nature of a law.

Third Article

WHETHER THE REASON OF ANY MAN IS COMPETENT TO MAKE LAWS?

We proceed thus to the Third Article:—

Objection 1. It would seem that the reason of any man is competent to make laws. For the Apostle says (Rom. ii. 14) that *when the Gentiles, who have not the law, do by nature those things that are of the law, . . . they are a law to themselves.* Now he says this of all in general. Therefore anyone can make a law for himself.

Obj. 2. Further, as the Philosopher says (*Ethic.* ii. 1), *the intention of the lawgiver is to lead men to virtue.* But every man can lead another to virtue. Therefore the reason of any man is competent to make laws.

Obj. 3. Further, just as the sovereign of a state governs the state, so every father of a family governs his household. But the sovereign of a state can make laws for the state. Therefore every father of a family can make laws for his household.

On the contrary, Isidore says (*Etym.* v. 10): *A law is an ordinance of the people whereby something is sanctioned by the Elders together with the Commonalty.*

I answer that, A law, properly speaking, regards first and foremost the order to the common good. Now to order anything to the common good, belongs either to the whole people, or to someone who is the vicegerent of the whole people. And therefore the making of a law belongs either to the whole people or to a public personage who has care of the whole people: since in all other matters the directing of anything to the end concerns him to whom the end belongs.

Reply Obj. 1. As stated above (A. 1 *ad* 1), a law is in a person not only as in one that rules, but also by participation as in one that is ruled. In the latter way each one is a law to himself, in so far as he shares the direction that he receives from one who rules him. Hence the same text goes on: *Who show the work of the law written in their hearts.*

Reply Obj. 2. A private person cannot lead another to virtue efficaciously: for he can only advise, and if his advice be not taken, it has no coercive power, such as the law should have, in order to prove an efficacious inducement to virtue, as the Philosopher says (*Ethic.* x. 9). But this coercive power is vested in the whole people or in some public personage, to whom it belongs to inflict penalties, as we shall state further on (Q. XCII., A. 2 *ad* 3; II-II., Q. LXIV., A. 3). Wherefore the framing of laws belongs to him alone.

Reply Obj. 3. As one man is a part of the household, so a household is a part of the state: and the state is a perfect community, according to *Polit.* i. 1. And therefore, as the good of one man is not the last end, but is ordained to the common good; so too the good of one household is ordained to the good of a single state, which is a perfect community. Consequently he that governs a family, can indeed make certain commands or ordinances, but not such as to have properly the force of law.

Fourth Article

WHETHER PROMULGATION IS ESSENTIAL TO A LAW?

We proceed thus to the Fourth Article:—
Objection 1. It would seem that promulgation is

not essential to a law. For the natural law above all has the character of law. But the natural law needs no promulgation. Therefore it is not essential to a law that it be promulgated.

Obj. 2. Further, it belongs properly to a law to bind one to do or not to do something. But the obligation of fulfilling a law touches not only those in whose presence it is promulgated, but also others. Therefore promulgation is not essential to a law.

Obj. 3. Further, the binding force of a law extends even to the future, since *laws are binding in matters of the future,* as the jurists say (*Cod.* I., tit. *De lege et constit.* leg. vii.). But promulgation concerns those who are present. Therefore it is not essential to a law.

On the contrary, It is laid down in the *Decretals,* dist. 4, that *laws are established when they are promulgated.*

I answer that, As stated above (A. 1), a law is imposed on others by way of a rule and measure. Now a rule or measure is imposed by being applied to those who are to be ruled and measured by it. Wherefore, in order that a law obtain the binding force which is proper to a law, it must needs be applied to the men who have to be ruled by it. Such application is made by its being notified to them by promulgation. Wherefore promulgation is necessary for the law to obtain its force.

Thus from the four preceding articles, the definition of law may be gathered; and it is nothing else than an ordinance of reason for the common good, made by him who has care of the community, and promulgated.

Reply Obj. 1. The natural law is promulgated by the very fact that God instilled it into man's mind so as to be known by him naturally.

Reply Obj. 2. Those who are not present when a law is promulgated, are bound to observe the law, in so far as it is notified or can be notified to them by others, after it has been promulgated.

Reply Obj. 3. The promulgation that takes place now, extends to future time by reason of the durability of written characters, by which means it is continually promulgated. Hence Isidore says (*Etym.* v. 3; ii. 10) that *lex* (law) *is derived from legere* (to read) *because it is written.*

QUESTION 91

OF THE VARIOUS KINDS OF LAW

(In Six Articles)

WE must now consider the various kinds of law: under which head there are six points of inquiry: (1) Whether there is an eternal law? (2) Whether there is a natural law? (3) Whether there is a human law? (4) Whether there is a Divine law? (5) Whether there is one Divine law, or several? (6) Whether there is a law of sin?

First Article

WHETHER THERE IS AN ETERNAL LAW?

We proceed thus to the First Article:—

Objection 1. It would seem that there is no eternal law. Because every law is imposed on someone. But there was not someone from eternity on whom a law could be imposed: since God alone was from eternity. Therefore no law is eternal.

Obj. 2. Further, promulgation is essential to law. But promulgation could not be from eternity: because there was no one to whom it could be promulgated from eternity. Therefore no law can be eternal.

Obj. 3. Further, a law implies order to an end. But nothing ordained to an end is eternal: for the last end alone is eternal. Therefore no law is eternal.

On the contrary, Augustine says (*De Lib. Arb.* i. 6): *That Law which is the Supreme Reason cannot be understood to be otherwise than unchangeable and eternal.*

I answer that, As stated above (Q. XC., A. 1 *ad* 2; AA. 3, 4), a law is nothing else but a dictate of practical reason emanating from the ruler who governs a perfect community. Now it is evident, granted that the world is ruled by Divine Providence, as was stated in the First Part (Q. XXII., AA. 1, 2), that the whole community of the universe is governed by Divine Reason. Wherefore the very Idea of the government of things in God the Ruler of the universe, has the nature of a law. And since the Divine Reason's conception of things is not subject to time but is eternal, according to Prov. viii. 23, therefore it is that this kind of law must be called eternal.

Reply Obj. 1. Those things that are not in themselves, exist with God, inasmuch as they are foreknown and pre-ordained by Him, according to Rom. iv. 17: *Who calls those things that are not, as those that are.* Accordingly the eternal concept of the Divine law bears the character of an eternal law, in so far as it is ordained by God to the government of things foreknown by Him.

Reply Obj. 2. Promulgation is made by word of mouth or in writing; and in both ways the eternal law is promulgated: because both the Divine Word and the writing of the Book of Life are eternal. But the promulgation cannot be from eternity on the part of the creature that hears or reads.

Reply Obj. 3. The law implies order to the end actively, in so far as it directs certain things to the end; but not passively,—that is to say, the law itself is not ordained to the end,—except accidentally, in a governor whose end is extrinsic to him, and to which end his law must needs be ordained. But the end of the Divine government is God Himself, and His law is not distinct from Himself. Wherefore the eternal law is not ordained to another end.

WHETHER THERE IS A NATURAL LAW?

We proceed thus to the Second Article:—
Objection 1. It would seem that there is no natural law in us. Because man is governed sufficiently by the eternal law: for Augustine says (*De Lib. Arb.* i) that *the eternal law is that by which it is right that all things should be most orderly.* But nature does not abound in superfluities as neither does she fail in necessaries. Therefore no law is natural to man.

Obj. 2. Further, by the law man is directed, in his acts, to the end, as stated above (Q. XC., A. 2). But the directing of human acts to their end is not a function of nature, as is the case in irrational creatures, which act for an end solely by their natural appetite; whereas man acts for an end by his reason and will. Therefore no law is natural to man.

Obj. 3. Further, the more a man is free, the less is he under the law. But man is freer than all the animals, on account of his free-will, with which he is endowed above all other animals. Since therefore other animals are not subject to a natural law, neither is man subject to a natural law.

On the contrary, A gloss on Rom. ii. 14: *When the Gentiles, who have not the law, do by nature those things that are of the law,* comments as follows: *Although they have no written law, yet they*

*have the natural law, whereby each one knows, and
is conscious of, what is good and what is evil.*

I answer that, As stated above (Q. XC., A. 1 *ad*
1), law, being a rule and measure, can be in a person
in two ways: in one way, as in him that rules and
measures; in another way, as in that which is ruled
and measured, since a thing is ruled and measured, in
so far as it partakes of the rule or measure. Wherefore, since all things subject to Divine providence
are ruled and measured by the eternal law, as was
stated above (A. 1); it is evident that all things
partake somewhat of the eternal law, in so far as,
namely, from its being imprinted on them, they
derive their respective inclinations to their proper
acts and ends. Now among all others, the rational
creature is subject to Divine providence in the most
excellent way, in so far as it partakes of a share of
providence, by being provident both for itself and
for others. Wherefore it has a share of the Eternal
Reason, whereby it has a natural inclination to its
proper act and end: and this participation of the
eternal law in the rational creature is called the
natural law. Hence the Psalmist after saying (Ps. iv.
6): *Offer up the sacrifice of justice,* as though someone asked what the works of justice are, adds: *Many
say, Who showeth us good things?* in answer to
which question he says: *The light of Thy counten-
ance, O Lord, is signed upon us:* thus implying that
the light of natural reason, whereby we discern what
is good and what is evil, which is the function of the
natural law, is nothing else than an imprint on us of

the Divine light. It is therefore evident that the natural law is nothing else than the rational creature's participation of the eternal law.

Reply Obj. 1. This argument would hold, if the natural law were something different from the eternal law: whereas it is nothing but a participation thereof, as stated above.

Reply Obj. 2. Every act of reason and will in us is based on that which is according to nature, as stated above (Q. X., A. 1): for every act of reasoning is based on principles that are known naturally, and every act of appetite in respect of the means is derived from the natural appetite in respect of the last end. Accordingly the first direction of our acts to their end must needs be in virtue of the natural law.

Reply Obj. 3. Even irrational animals partake in their own way of the Eternal Reason, just as the rational creature does. But because the rational creature partakes thereof in an intellectual and rational manner, therefore the participation of the eternal law in the rational creature is properly called a law, since a law is something pertaining to reason, as stated above (Q. XC., A. 1). Irrational creatures, however, do not partake thereof in a rational manner, wherefore there is no participation of the eternal law in them, except by way of similitude.

THIRD ARTICLE

WHETHER THERE IS A HUMAN LAW?

We proceed thus to the Third Article:—

Objection 1. It would seem that there is not a human law. For the natural law is a participation of the eternal law, as stated above (A. 2). Now through the eternal law *all things are most orderly,* as Augustine states (*De Lib. Arb.* i. 6). Therefore the natural law suffices for the ordering of all human affairs. Consequently there is no need for a human law.

Obj. 2. Further, a law bears the character of a measure, as stated above (Q. XC., A. 1). But human reason is not a measure of things, but vice versa, as stated in *Metaph.* x., text 5. Therefore no law can emanate from human reason.

Obj. 3. Further a measure should be most certain, as stated in *Metaph.* x., text. 3. But the dictates of human reason in matters of conduct are uncertain, according to Wis. ix. 14: *The thoughts of mortal men are fearful, and our counsels uncertain.* Therefore no law can emanate from human reason.

On the contrary, Augustine (*De Lib. Arb.* i. 6), distinguishes two kinds of law, the one eternal, the other temporal, which he calls human.

I answer that, As stated above (Q. XC., A. 1 *ad* 2), a law is a dictate of the practical reason. Now it is to be observed that the same procedure takes place in the practical and in the speculative reason: for each proceeds from principles to conclusions, as stated above (*ibid.*). Accordingly we conclude that just as, in the speculative reason, from naturally known indemonstrable principles, we draw the conclusions of the various sciences, the knowledge of which is not imparted to us by nature, but acquired by the efforts of reason, so too it is from the precepts of the natural law, as from general and indemonstrable principles, that the human reason needs to proceed to the more particular determination of certain matters. These particular determinations, devised by human reason, are called human laws, provided the other essential conditions of law be observed, as stated above (Q. XC., AA. 2, 3, 4). Wherefore Tully says in his *Rhetoric* (*De Invent. Rhet.* ii.) that *justice has its source in nature; thence certain things came into custom by reason of their utility; afterwards these things which emanated from nature and were approved by custom, were sanctioned by fear and reverence for the law.*

Reply Obj. 1. The human reason cannot have a full participation of the dictate of the Divine Reason, but according to its own mode, and imperfectly. Consequently, as on the part of the speculative reason, by a natural participation of Divine Wisdom, there is in us the knowledge of certain general principles, but not proper knowledge of each single truth, such as that contained in the Divine Wisdom; so too, on the part of the practical reason, man has a natural participation of the eternal law, according to certain general principles, but not as regards the particular determinations of individual cases, which are, however, contained in the eternal law. Hence the need for human reason to proceed further to sanction them by law.

Reply Obj. 2. Human reason is not, of itself, the rule of things: but the principles impressed on it by nature, are general rules and measures of all things relating to human conduct, whereof the natural reason is the rule and measure, although it is not the measure of things that are from nature.

Reply Obj. 3. The practical reason is concerned with practical matters, which are singular and contingent: but not with necessary things, with which the speculative reason is concerned. Wherefore human laws cannot have that inerrancy that belongs to the demonstrated conclusions of sciences. Nor is it necessary for every measure to be altogether unerring and certain, but according as it is possible in its own particular genus.

FOURTH ARTICLE

WHETHER THERE WAS ANY NEED FOR A DIVINE LAW?

We proceed thus to the Fourth Article:—

Objection 1. It would seem that there was no need for a Divine law. Because, as stated above (A. 2), the natural law is a participation in us of the eternal law. But the eternal law is a Divine law, as stated above (A. 1). Therefore there is no need for a Divine law in addition to the natural law, and human laws derived therefrom.

Obj. 2. Further, it is written (Ecclus. xv. 14) that *God left man in the hand of his own counsel.* Now counsel is an act of reason, as stated above (Q. XIV., A. 1). Therefore man was left to the direction of his reason. But a dictate of human reason is a human law, as stated above (A. 3). Therefore there is no need for man to be governed also by a Divine law.

Obj. 3. Further, human nature is more self-sufficing than irrational creatures. But irrational creatures have no Divine law besides the natural inclination impressed on them. Much less, therefore, should the rational creature have a Divine law in addition to the natural law.

On the contrary, David prayed God to set His law before him, saying (Ps. cxviii. 33): *Set before me for a law the way of Thy justifications, O Lord.*

I answer that, Besides the natural and the human law it was necessary for the directing of human conduct to have a Divine law. And this for four reasons. First, because it is by law that man is directed how to perform his proper acts in view of his last end. And indeed if man were ordained to no other end than that which is proportionate to his natural faculty, there would be no need for man to have any further direction on the part of his reason, besides the natural law and human law which is derived from it. But since man is ordained to an end of eternal happiness which is inproportionate to man's natural faculty, as stated above (Q. V., A. 5), therefore it was necessary that, besides the natural and the human law, man should be directed to his end by a law given by God.

Secondly, because, on account of the uncertainty of human judgment, especially on contingent and particular matters, different people form different judgments on human acts; whence also different and contrary laws result. In order, therefore, that man may know without any doubt what he ought to do and what he ought to avoid, it was necessary for man to be directed in his proper acts by a law given by God, for it is certain that such a law cannot err.

Thirdly, because man can make laws in those matters of which he is competent to judge. But man is not competent to judge of interior movements, that are hidden, but only of exterior acts which appear: and yet for the perfection of virtue it is necessary for man to conduct himself aright in both kinds of acts. Consequently human law could not sufficiently curb and direct interior acts; and it was necessary for this purpose that a Divine law should supervene.

Fourthly, because, as Augustine says (*De Lib. Arb.* i. 5, 6), human law cannot punish or forbid all evil deeds: since while aiming at doing away with all evils, it would do away with many good things, and would hinder the advance of the common good, which is necessary for human intercourse. In order therefore, that no evil might remain unforbidden and unpunished, it was necessary for the Divine law to supervene, whereby all sins are forbidden.

And these four causes are touched upon in Ps. cxviii. 8, where it is said: *The law of the Lord is unspotted*, i.e., allowing no foulness of sin; *converting souls*, because it directs not only exterior, but also interior acts; *the testimony of the Lord is faithful*, because of the certainty of what is true and right; *giving wisdom to little ones*, by directing man to an end supernatural and Divine.

Reply Obj. 1. By the natural law the eternal law is participated proportionately to the capacity of human nature. But to his supernatural end man needs to be directed in a yet higher way. Hence the additional law given by God, whereby man shares more perfectly in the eternal law.

Reply Obj. 2. Counsel is a kind of inquiry: hence it must proceed from some principles. Nor is it enough for it to proceed from principles imparted by nature, which are the precepts of the natural law, for the reasons given above: but there is need for certain additional principles, namely, the precepts of the Divine law.

Reply Obj. 3. Irrational creatures are not ordained to an end higher than that which is proportionate to their natural powers: consequently the comparison fails.

FIFTH ARTICLE

WHETHER THERE IS BUT ONE DIVINE LAW?

We proceed thus to the Fifth Article:—

Objection 1. It would seem that there is but one Divine law. Because, where there is one king in one kingdom there is but one law. Now the whole of mankind is compared to God as to one king, according to Ps. xlvi. 8: *God is King of all the earth.* Therefore there is but one Divine law.

Obj. 2. Further, every law is directed to the end which the lawgiver intends for those for whom he makes the law. But God intends one and the same thing for all men; since according to 1 Tim. ii. 4: *He will have all men to be saved, and to come to the knowledge of the truth.* Therefore there is but one Divine law.

Obj. 3. Further, the Divine law seems to be more akin to the eternal law, which is one, than the natural law, according as the revelation of grace is of a higher order than natural knowledge. Therefore much more is the Divine law but one.

On the contrary. The Apostle says (Heb. vii. 12): *The priesthood being translated, it is necessary that a translation also be made of the law.* But the priesthood is twofold, as stated in the same passage, viz., the levitical priesthood, and the priesthood of Christ. Therefore the Divine law is twofold, namely, the Old Law and the New Law.

I answer that, As stated in the First Part (Q. XXX., A. 3), distinction is the cause of number. Now things may be distinguished in two ways. First, as those things that are altogether specifically different, *e.g.*, a horse and an ox. Secondly, as perfect and imperfect in the same species, *e.g.*, a boy and a man: and in this way the Divine law is divided into Old and New. Hence the Apostle (Gal. iii. 24, *25) compares the state of man under the Old Law to that of a child *under a pedagogue;* but the state under the New Law, to that of a full grown man, who is *no longer under a pedagogue.*

Now the perfection and imperfection of these two laws is to be taken in connection with the three conditions pertaining to law, as stated above. For, in the first place, it belongs to law to be directed to the common good as to its end, as stated above (Q. XC., A. 2). This good may be twofold. It may be a sensible and earthly good; and to this, man was directly ordained by the Old Law: wherefore, at the very outset of the law, the people were invited to the earthly kingdom of the Chananaeans (Exod. iii. 8, 17). Again it may be an intelligible and heavenly good: and to this, man is ordained by the New Law. Wherefore, at the very beginning of His preaching, Christ invited men to the kingdom of heaven, saying (Matth. iv. 17): *Do penance, for the kingdom of heaven is at hand.* Hence Augustine says (*Contra*

Faust. iv.) that *promises of temporal goods are contained in the Old Testament, for which reason it is called old; but the promise of eternal life belongs to the New Testament.*

Secondly, it belongs to the law to direct human acts according to the order of righteousness (A. 4): wherein also the New Law surpasses the Old Law, since it directs our internal acts, according to Matth. v. 20: *Unless your justice abound more than that of the Scribes and Pharisees, you shall not enter into the kingdom of heaven.* Hence the saying that *the Old Law restrains the hand, but the New Law controls the mind* (3 *Sentent.*, D. xl.).

Thirdly, it belongs to the law to induce men to observe its commandments. This the Old Law did by the fear of punishment: but the New Law, by love, which is poured into our hearts by the grace of Christ, bestowed in the New Law, but foreshadowed in the Old. Hence Augustine says (*Contra Adimant. Manich. discip.* xvii.) that *there is little difference* between the Law and the Gospel—fear and love.*

Reply Obj. 1. As the father of a family issues different commands to the children and to the adults, so also the one King, God, in his one kingdom, gave one law to men, while they were yet imperfect, and another more perfect law, when, by the preceding law, they had been led to a greater capacity for Divine things.

Reply Obj. 2. The salvation of man could not be

---

* The *little difference* refers to the Latin words *timor* and *amor,—fear* and *love.*

achieved otherwise than through Christ, according to Acts iv. 12: *There is no other name . . . given to men, whereby we must be saved.* Consequently the law that brings all to salvation could not be given until after the coming of Christ. But before His coming it was necessary to give to the people, of whom Christ was to be born, a law containing certain rudiments of righteousness unto salvation, in order to prepare them to receive Him.

Reply Obj. 3. The natural law directs man by way of certain general precepts, common to both the perfect and the imperfect: wherefore it is one and the same for all. But the Divine law directs man also in certain particular matters, to which the perfect and imperfect do not stand in the same relation. Hence the necessity for the Divine law to be twofold, as already explained.

Sixth Article

WHETHER THERE IS A LAW IN THE FOMES OF SIN?

We proceed thus to the Sixth Article:—

Objection 1. It would seem that there is no law of the 'fomes' of sin. For Isidore says (*Etym.* v.) that the *law is based on reason.* But the 'fomes' of sin is not based on reason, but deviates from it. Therefore the 'fomes' has not the nature of a law.

Obj. 2. Further, every law is binding, so that those

who do not obey it are called transgressors. But man is not called a transgressor, from not following the instigations of the 'fomes'; but rather from his following them. Therefore the 'fomes' has not the nature of a law.

Obj. 3. Further, the law is ordained to the common good, as stated above (Q. XC., A. 2). But the 'fomes' inclines us, not to the common, but to our own private good. Therefore the 'fomes' has not the nature of sin.

On the contrary, The Apostle says (Rom. vii. 23): *I see another law in my members, fighting against the law of my mind.*

I answer that, As stated above (A. 2; Q. XC., A. 1 *ad* 1), the law, as to its essence, resides in him that rules and measures; but, by way of participation, in that which is ruled and measured; so that every inclination or ordination which may be found in things subject to the law, is called a law by participation, as stated above (*ibid.*). Now those who are subject to a law may receive a twofold inclination from the lawgiver. First, in so far as he directly inclines his subjects to something; sometimes indeed different subjects to different acts; in this way we may say that there is a military law and a mercantile law. Secondly, indirectly; thus by the very fact that a lawgiver deprives a subject of some dignity, the latter passes into another order, so as to be under another law, as it were: thus if a soldier be turned out of the army, he becomes a subject of rural or of mercantile legislation.

Accordingly under the Divine Lawgiver various
creatures have various natural inclinations, so that
what is, as it were, a law for one, is against the law
for another: thus I might say that fierceness is, in a
way, the law of a dog, but against the law of a sheep
or another meek animal. And so the law of man,
which, by the Divine ordinance, is alloted to him,
according to his proper natural condition, is that he
should act in accordance with reason: and this law
was so effective in the primitive state, that nothing
either beside or against reason could take man un-
awares. But when man turned his back on God, he
fell under the influence of his sensual impulses: in
fact this happens to each one individually, the more
he deviates from the path of reason, so that, after
a fashion, he is likened to the beasts that are led by
the impulse of sensuality, according to Ps. xlviii. 21:
*Man, when he was in honour, did not understand:
he hath been compared to senseless beasts, and made
like to them.*

So, then, this very inclination of sensuality which
is called the 'fomes,' in other animals has simply the
nature of a law, (yet only in so far as a law may be
said to be in such things), by reason of a direct
inclination. But in man, it has not the nature of law
in this way, rather is it a deviation from the law
of reason. But since, by the just sentence of God,
man is destitute of original justice, and his reason
bereft of its vigour, this impulse of sensuality,
whereby he is led, in so far as it is a penalty follow-

ing from the Divine law depriving man of his proper dignity, has the nature of a law.

Reply Obj. 1. This argument considers the 'fomes' in itself, as an incentive to evil. It is not thus that it has the nature of a law, as stated above, but according as it results from the justice of the Divine law: it is as though we were to say that the law allows a nobleman to be condemned to hard labour for some misdeed.

Reply Obj. 2. This argument considers law in the light of a rule or measure: for it is in this sense that those who deviate from the law become transgressors. But the 'fomes' is not a law in this respect, but by a kind of participation, as stated above.

Reply Obj. 3. This argument considers the 'fomes' as to its proper inclination, and not as to its origin. And yet if the inclination of sensuality be considered as it is in other animals, thus it is ordained to the common good, namely, to the preservation of nature in the species or in the individual. And this is in man also, in so far as sensuality is subject to reason. But it is called the 'fomes' in so far as it strays from the order of reason.

OF THE EFFECTS OF LAW

(*In Two Articles*)

WE must now consider the effects of law; under
which head there are two points of inquiry: (1)
Whether an effect of law is to make men good? (2)
Whether the effects of law are to command, to forbid, to permit, and to punish, as the Jurist states?

FIRST ARTICLE

WHETHER AN EFFECT OF LAW IS TO MAKE MEN GOOD?

We proceed thus to the First Article:—
Objection 1. It seems that it is not an effect of
law to make men good. For men are good through
virtue, since virtue, as stated in *Ethic.* ii. 6 is *that
which makes its subject good*. But virtue is in man
from God alone, because He it is Who *works it in
us without us*, as we stated above (Q. LV., A. 4)
in giving the. definition of virtue. Therefore the law
does not make men good.

Obj. 2. Further, Law does not profit a man unless
he obeys it. But the very fact that a man obeys a
law is due to his being good. Therefore in man good-

ness is presupposed to the law. Therefore the law does
not make men good.

Obj. 3. Further, Law is ordained to the common
good, as stated above (Q. XC., A. 2). But some behave well in things regarding the community, who
behave ill in things regarding themselves. Therefore
it is not the business of the law to make men good.

Obj. 4. Further, some laws are tyrannical, as the
Philosopher says (*Polit.* iii. 6). But a tyrant does not
intend the good of his subjects, but considers only
his own profit. Therefore law does not make men
good.

On the contrary, The Philosopher says (*Ethic.* ii.
1) that the *intention of every lawgiver is to make
good citizens.*

I answer that, As stated above (Q. XC., A. 1 *ad* 2;
AA. 3, 4), a law is nothing else than a dictate of
reason in the ruler by whom his subjects are governed.
Now the virtue of any subordinate thing consists in
its being well subordinated to that by which it is
regulated: thus we see that the virtue of the irascible and concupiscible faculties consists in their
being obedient to reason; and accordingly *the virtue
of every subject consists in his being well subjected
to his ruler,* as the Philosopher says (*Polit.* i.). But
every law aims at being obeyed by those who are
subject to it. Consequently it is evident that the
proper effect of law is to lead its subjects to their
proper virtue: and since virtue is *that which makes
its subject good,* it follows that the proper effect of
law is to make those to whom it is given, good,

either simply or in some particular respect. For if the intention of the lawgiver is fixed on true good, which is the common good regulated according to Divine justice, it follows that the effect of the law is to make men good simply. If, however, the intention of the lawgiver is fixed on that which is not simply good, but useful or pleasurable to himself, or in opposition to Divine justice; then the law does not make men good simply, but in respect to that particular government. In this way good is found even in things that are bad of themselves: thus a man is called a good robber, because he works in a way that is adapted to his end.

Reply Obj. 1. Virtue is twofold, as explained above (Q. LXIII., A. 2), viz., acquired and infused. Now the fact of being accustomed to an action contributes to both, but in different ways; for it causes the acquired virtue; while it disposes to infused virtue, and preserves and fosters it when it already exists. And since law is given for the purpose of directing human acts; as far as human acts conduce to virtue, so far does law make men good. Wherefore the Philosopher says in the second book of the *Politics* (*Ethic.* ii.) that *lawgivers make men good by habituating them to good works.*

Reply Obj. 2. It is not always through perfect goodness of virtue that one obeys the law, but sometimes it is through fear of punishment, and sometimes from the mere dictate of reason, which is a beginning of virtue, as stated above (Q. LXIII., A. 1).

Reply Obj. 3. The goodness of any part is considered in comparison with the whole; hence Augustine says (*Conf.* iii.) that *unseemly is the part that harmonizes not with the whole.* Since then every man is a part of the state, it is impossible that a man be good, unless he be well proportionate to the common good: nor can the whole be well consistent unless its parts be proportionate to it. Consequently the common good of the state cannot flourish, unless the citizens be virtuous, at least those whose business it is to govern. But it is enough for the good of the community, that the other citizens be so far virtuous that they obey the commands of their rulers. Hence the Philosopher says (*Polit.* iii. 2) that *the virtue of a sovereign is the same as that of a good man, but the virtue of any common citizen is not the same as that of a good man.*

Reply Obj. 4. A tyrannical law, through not being according to reason, is not a law, absolutely speaking, but rather a perversion of law; and yet in so far as it is something in the nature of a law, it aims at the citizens being good. For all it has in the nature of a law consists in its being an ordinance made by a superior to his subjects, and aims at being obeyed by them, which is to make them good, not simply, but with respect to that particular government.

Second Article

WHETHER THE ACTS OF LAW ARE SUITABLY ASSIGNED?

We proceed thus to the Second Article:—

Objection 1. It would seem that the acts of law are not suitably assigned as consisting in *command, prohibition, permission* and *punishment*. For *every law is a general precept,* as the jurist states (*ibid.*) But command and precept are the same. Therefore the other three are superfluous.

Obj. 2. Further, the effect of a law is to induce its subjects to be good, as stated above (A. 1). But counsel aims at a higher good than a command does. Therefore it belongs to law to counsel rather than to command.

Obj. 3. Further, just as punishment stirs a man to good deeds, so does reward. Therefore if to punish is reckoned an effect of law, so also is to reward.

Obj. 4. Further, the intention of a lawgiver is to make men good, as stated above (A. 1). But he that obeys the law, merely through fear of being punished, is not good: because *although a good deed may be done through servile fear,* i.e., *fear of punishment, it is not done well,* as Augustine says (*Contra duas Epist. Pelag.* ii.). Therefore punishment is not a proper effect of law.

On the contrary, Isidore says (*Etym.* v. 19): *Every*

law either permits something, as: 'A brave man may demand his reward': or forbids something, as: 'No man may ask a consecrated virgin in marriage': or punishes, as: 'Let him that commits a murder be put to death.'

I answer that, Just as an assertion is a dictate of reason asserting something, so is a law a dictate of reason, commanding something. Now it is proper to reason to lead from one thing to another. Wherefore just as, in demonstrative sciences, the reason leads us from certain principles to assent to the conclusion, so it induces us by some means to assent to the precept of the law.

Now the precepts of law are concerned with human acts, in which the law directs, as stated above (Q. XC., AA. 1, 2; Q. XCI., A. 4). Again, there are three kinds of human acts: for, as stated above (Q. XVIII., A. 8), some acts are good generically, viz., acts of virtue; and in respect of these the act of the law is a precept or command, for *the law commands all acts of virtue* (*Ethic.* v. 1). Some acts are evil generically, viz., acts of vice, and in respect of these the law forbids. Some acts are generically indifferent, and in respect of these the law permits; and all acts that are either not distinctly good or not distinctly bad may be called indifferent.—And it is the fear of punishment that law makes use of in order to ensure obedience: in which respect punishment is an effect of law.

Reply Obj. 1. Just as to cease from evil is a kind of good, so a prohibition is a kind of precept: and accordingly, taking precept in a wide sense, every law is a kind of precept.

Reply Obj. 2. To advise is not a proper act of law, but may be within the competency even of a private person, who cannot make a law. Wherefore too the Apostle, after giving a certain counsel (1 Cor. vii. 12) says: *I speak, not the Lord.* Consequently it is not reckoned as an effect of law.

Reply Obj. 3. To reward may also pertain to anyone: but to punish pertains to none but the framer of the law, by whose authority the pain is inflicted. Wherefore to reward is not reckoned an effect of law, but only to punish.

Reply Obj. 4. From becoming accustomed to avoid evil and fulfil what is good, through fear of punishment, one is sometimes led on to do so likewise, with delight and of one's own accord. Accordingly, law, even by punishing, leads men on to being good.

QUESTION 93

OF THE ETERNAL LAW

(*In Six Articles*)

WE must now consider each law by itself; and (1) The eternal law: (2) The natural law: (3) The human law: (4) The old law: (5) The new law, which is the law of the Gospel. Of the sixth law which is the law of the 'fomes,' suffice what we have said when treating of original sin.

Concerning the first there are six points of inquiry: (1) What is the eternal law? (2) Whether it is known to all? (3) Whether every law is derived from it? (4) Whether necessary things are subject to the eternal law? (5) Whether natural contingencies are subject to the eternal law? (6) Whether all human things are subject to it?

FIRST ARTICLE

WHETHER THE ETERNAL LAW IS A SOVEREIGN TYPE* EXISTING IN GOD?

We proceed thus to the First Article:—
Objection 1. It would seem that the eternal law is not a sovereign type existing in God. For there is only one eternal law. But there are many types of things in the Divine mind; for Augustine says (*Qq.* lxxxiii., qu. 46) that God *made each thing according to its type*. Therefore the eternal law does not seem to be a type existing in the Divine mind.

Obj. 2. Further, it is essential to a law that it be promulgated by word, as stated above (Q. XC., A. 4). But Word is a Personal name in God, as stated in the First Part (Q. XXXIV., A. 1): whereas type refers to the Essence. Therefore the eternal law is not the same as a Divine type.

Obj. 3. Further, Augustine says (*De Vera Relig.* xxx.): *We see a law above our minds, which is*

* Ratio.

called truth. But the law which is above our minds
is the eternal law. Therefore truth is the eternal law.
But the idea of truth is not the same as the idea of
a type. Therefore the eternal law is not the same as
the sovereign type.

On the contrary, Augustine says (*De Lib. Arb.* i.
6) that *the eternal law is the sovereign type, to
which we must always conform.*

I answer that, Just as in every artificer there pre-
exists a type of the things that are made by his art,
so too in every governor there must pre-exist the type
of the order of those things that are to be done by
those who are subject to his government. And just
as the type of the things yet to be made by an art is
called the art or exemplar of the products of that
art, so too the type in him who governs the acts of
his subjects, bears the character of a law, provided
the other conditions be present which we have mentioned above (Q. XC.). Now God, by His wisdom,
is the Creator of all things, in relation to which He
stands as the artificer to the products of his art, as
stated in the First Part (Q. XIV., A. 8). Moreover
He governs all the acts and movements that are to
be found in each single creature, as was also stated
in the First Part (Q. CIII., A. 5). Wherefore as the
type of the Divine Wisdom, inasmuch as by It all
things are created, has the character of art, exemplar
or idea; so the type of Divine Wisdom, as moving all
things to their due end, bears the character of law.
Accordingly the eternal law is nothing else than the

type of Divine Wisdom, as directing all actions and movements.

Reply Obj. 1. Augustine is speaking in that passage of the ideal types which regard the proper nature of each single thing; and consequently in them there is a certain distinction and plurality, according to their different relations to things, as stated in the First Part (Q. XV., A. 2). But law is said to direct human acts by ordaining them to the common good, as stated above (Q. XC., A. 2). And things, which are in themselves different, may be considered as one, according as they are ordained to one common thing. Wherefore the eternal law is one since it is the type of this order.

Reply Obj. 2. With regard to any sort of word, two points may be considered: viz., the word itself, and that which is expressed by the word. For the spoken word is something uttered by the mouth of man, and expresses that which is signified by the human word. The same applies to the human mental word, which is nothing else than something conceived by the mind, by which man expresses his thoughts mentally. So then in God the Word conceived by the intellect of the Father is the name of a Person: but all things that are in the Father's knowledge, whether they refer to the Essence or to the Persons, or to the works of God, are expressed by this Word, as Augustine declares (*De Trin.* xv. 14). And among other things expressed by this Word, the eternal law itself is expressed thereby. Nor does it follow that the eternal law is a Personal name in God: yet it is appropriated to the Son, on account of the kinship between type and word.

Reply Obj. 3. The types of the Divine intellect do not stand in the same relation to things, as the types of the human intellect. For the human intellect is measured by things, so that a human concept is not true by reason of itself, but by reason of its being consonant with things, since *an opinion is true or false according as it answers to the reality.* But the Divine intellect is the measure of things: since each thing has so far truth in it, as it represents the Divine intellect, as was stated in the First Part (Q. XVI., A. 1). Consequently the Divine intellect is true in itself; and its type is truth itself.

SECOND ARTICLE

WHETHER THE ETERNAL LAW IS KNOWN TO ALL?

We proceed thus to the Second Article:—

Objection 1. It would seem that the eternal law is not known to all. Because, as the Apostle says (1 Cor. ii. 11), *the things that are of God no man knoweth, but the Spirit of God.* But the eternal law is a type existing in the Divine mind. Therefore it is unknown to all save God alone.

Obj. 2. Further, as Augustine says (*De Lib. Arb.* i. 6) *the eternal law is that by which it is right that all things should be most orderly.* But all do not know how all things are most orderly. Therefore all do not know the eternal law.

Obj. 3. Further, Augustine says (*De Vera Relig.* xxxi.) that *the eternal law is not subject to the judgment of man.* But according to *Ethic.* i. *any man can judge well of what he knows.* Therefore the eternal law is not known to us.

On the contrary, Augustine says (*De Lib. Arb.* i. 6) that *knowledge of the eternal law is imprinted on us.*

I answer that, A thing may be known in two ways: first, in itself; secondly, in its effect, wherein some likeness of that thing is found: thus someone not seeing the sun in its substance, may know it by its rays. So then no one can know the eternal law, as it is in itself, except the blessed who see God in His Essence. But every rational creature knows it in its reflection, greater or less. For every knowledge of truth is a kind of reflection and participation of the eternal law, which is the unchangeable truth, as Augustine says (*De Vera Relig.* xxxi.). Now all men know the truth to a certain extent, at least as to the common principles of the natural law: and as to the others, they partake of the knowledge of truth, some more, some less; and in this respect are more or less cognizant of the eternal law.

Reply Obj. 1. We cannot know the things that are of God, as they are in themselves; but they are made known to us in their effects, according to Rom. i. 20: *The invisible things of God . . . are clearly seen, being understood by the things that are made.*

Reply Obj. 2. Although each one knows the eternal law according to his own capacity, in the way explained above, yet none can comprehend it: for it cannot be made perfectly known by its effects. Therefore it does not follow that anyone who knows the eternal law in the way aforesaid, knows also the whole order of things, whereby they are most orderly.

Reply Obj. 3. To judge of a thing may be understood in two ways. First, as when a cognitive power judges of its proper object, according to Job xii. 11: *Doth not the ear discern words, and the palate of him that eateth, the taste?* It is to this kind of judgment that the Philosopher alludes when he says that *anyone can judge well of what he knows,* by judging, namely, whether what is put forward is true. In another way we speak of a superior judging of a subordinate by a kind of practical judgment, as to whether he should be such and such or not. And thus none can judge of the eternal law.

THIRD ARTICLE

WHETHER EVERY LAW IS DERIVED FROM THE ETERNAL LAW?

We proceed thus to the Third Article:—

Objection 1. It would seem that not every law is derived from the eternal law. For there is a law of the 'fomes,' as stated above (Q. XCI., A. 6), which is not derived from that Divine law which is the eternal law, since thereunto pertains the *prudence of the flesh,* of which the Apostle says (Rom. viii. 7), that *it cannot be subject to the law of God.* Therefore not every law is derived from the eternal law.

Obj. 2. Further, nothing unjust can be derived from the external law, because, as stated above (A. 2, *Obj.* 2), *the eternal law is that, according to which it is right that all things should be most orderly.* But some laws are unjust, according to Isa. x. 1: *Woe to them that make wicked laws.* Therefore not every law is derived from the eternal law.

Obj. 3. Further, Augustine says (*De Lib. Arb.* i. 5) that *the law which is framed for ruling the people, rightly permits many things which are punished by Divine providence.* But the type of Divine providence is the eternal law, as stated above (A. 1). Therefore not even every good law is derived from the eternal law.

On the contrary, Divine Wisdom says (Prov. viii. 15): *By Me kings reign, and lawgivers decree just things.* But the type of Divine Wisdom is the eternal law, as stated above (A. 1). Therefore all laws proceed from the eternal law.

I answer that, As stated above (Q. XC., AA. 1, 2), law denotes a kind of plan directing acts towards an end. Now wherever there are movers ordained to one another, the power of the second mover must needs be derived from the power of the first mover; since the second mover does not move except in so far as it is moved by the first. Wherefore we observe

the same in all those who govern, so that the plan
of government is derived by secondary governors
from the governor in chief: thus the plan of what
is to be done in a state flows from the king's command to his inferior administrators: and again in
things of art the plan of whatever is to be done by
art flows from the chief craftsman to the under-
craftsmen who work with their hands. Since then
the eternal law is the plan of government in the Chief
Governor, all the plans of government in the inferior
governors must be derived from the eternal law. But
these plans of inferior governors are all other laws
besides the eternal law. Therefore all laws, in so far
as they partake of right reason, are derived from the
eternal law. Hence Augustine says (*De Lib. Arb.* i.
6) that *in temporal law there is nothing just and
lawful, but what man has drawn from the eternal
law.*

Reply Obj. 1. The 'fomes' has the nature of law
in man, in so far as it is a punishment resulting from
Divine justice; and in this respect it is evident that
it is derived from the eternal law. But in so far as it
denotes a proneness to sin, it is contrary to the Divine
law, and has not the nature of law, as stated above
(Q. XCI., A. 6).

Reply Obj. 2. Human law has the nature of law
in so far as it partakes of right reason; and it is
clear that, in this respect, it is derived from the
eternal law. But in so far as it deviates from reason,
it is called an unjust law, and has the nature, not
of law but of violence. Nevertheless even an unjust

law, in so far as it retains some appearance of law, though being framed by one who is in power, is derived from the eternal law; since all power is from the Lord God, according to Rom. xiii. 1.

Reply Obj. 3. Human law is said to permit certain things, not as approving of them, but as being unable to direct them. And many things are directed by the Divine law, which human law is unable to direct, because more things are subject to a higher than to a lower cause. Hence the very fact that human law does not meddle with matters it cannot direct, comes under the ordination of the eternal law. It would be different, were human law to sanction what the eternal law condemns. Consequently it does not follow that human law is not derived from the eternal law, but that it is not on a perfect equality with it.

FOURTH ARTICLE

WHETHER NECESSARY AND ETERNAL THINGS ARE SUBJECT TO THE ETERNAL LAW?

We proceed thus to the Fourth Article:—

Objection 1. It would seem that necessary and eternal things are subject to the eternal law. For whatever is reasonable is subject to reason. But the Divine will is reasonable, for it is just. Therefore it is subject to (the Divine) reason. But the eternal law is the Divine reason. Therefore God's will is subject to the eternal law. But God's will is eternal. Therefore eternal and necessary things are subject to the eternal law.

Obj. 2. Further, whatever is subject to the King, is subject to the King's law. Now the Son, according to 1 Cor. xv. 28, 24, *shall be subject . . . to God and the Father, . . . when He shall have delivered up the Kingdom to Him.* Therefore the Son, Who is eternal, is subject to the eternal law.

Obj. 3. Further, the eternal law is Divine providence as a type. But many necessary things are subject to Divine providence: for instance, the stability of incorporeal substances and of the heavenly bodies. Therefore even necessary things are subject to the eternal law.

On the contrary, Things that are necessary cannot be otherwise, and consequently need no restraining. But laws are imposed on men, in order to restrain them from evil, as explained above (Q. XCII., A. 2). Therefore necessary things are not subject to the eternal law.

I answer that, As stated above (A. 1), the eternal law is the type of the Divine government. Consequently whatever is subject to the Divine government, is subject to the eternal law: while if anything is not subject to the Divine government, neither is it subject to the eternal law. The application of this distinction may be gathered by looking around us. For those things are subject to human government, which can be done by man; but what pertains to the nature of man is not subject to human government;

for instance, that he should have a soul, hands, or feet. Accordingly all that is in things created by God, whether it be contingent or necessary, is subject to the eternal law: while things pertaining to the Divine Nature or Essence are not subject to the eternal law, but are the eternal law itself.

Reply Obj. 1. We may speak of God's will in two ways. First, as to the will itself: and thus, since God's will is His very Essence, it is subject neither to the Divine government, nor to the eternal law, but is the same thing as the eternal law. Secondly, we may speak of God's will, as to the things themselves that God wills about creatures; which things are subject to the eternal law, in so far as they are planned by Divine Wisdom. In reference to these things God's will is said to be reasonable (*rationalis*): though regarded in itself it should rather be called their type (*ratio*).

Reply Obj. 2. God the Son was not made by God, but was naturally born of God. Consequently He is not subject to Divine providence or to the eternal law: but rather is Himself the eternal law by a kind of appropriation, as Augustine explains (*De Vera Relig.* xxxi.). But He is said to be subject to the Father by reason of His human nature, in respect of which also the Father is said to be greater than He.

The third objection we grant, because it deals with those necessary things that are created.

Reply Obj. 4. As the Philosopher says (*Metaph.* v., text. 6), some necessary things have a cause of their necessity: and thus they derive from something else the fact that they cannot be otherwise. And this is in itself a most effective restraint; for whatever is restrained, is said to be restrained in so far as it cannot do otherwise than it is allowed to.

FIFTH ARTICLE

WHETHER NATURAL CONTINGENTS ARE SUBJECT TO THE ETERNAL LAW?

We proceed thus to the Fifth Article:—

Objection 1. It would seem that natural contingents are not subject to the eternal law. Because promulgation is essential to law, as stated above (Q. XC., A. 4). But a law cannot be promulgated except to rational creatures, to whom it is possible to make an announcement. Therefore none but rational creatures are subject to the eternal law; and consequently natural contingents are not.

Obj. 2. Further, *Whatever obeys reason partakes somewhat of reason,* as stated in *Ethic.* i. But the eternal law is the supreme type, as stated above (A. 1). Since then natural contingents do not partake of reason in any way, but are altogether void of reason, it seems that they are not subject to the eternal law.

Obj. 3. Further, the eternal law is most efficient. But in natural contingents defects occur. Therefore they are not subject to the eternal law.

On the contrary, It is written (Prov. viii. 29): *When He compassed the sea with its bounds, and set*

*a law to the waters, that they should not pass their
limits.*

I answer that, We must speak otherwise of the law
of man, than of the eternal law which is the law of
God. For the law of man extends only to rational
creatures subject to man. The reason of this is because
law directs the actions of those that are subject to
the government of someone; wherefore, properly
speaking, none imposes a law on his own actions.
Now whatever is done regarding the use of irrational
things subject to man, is done by the act of man
himself moving those things, for these irrational creatures do not move themselves, but are moved by
others, as stated above (Q. I., A. 2). Consequently
man cannot impose laws on irrational beings, however much they may be subject to him. But he can
impose laws on rational beings subject to him, in so
far as by his command or pronouncement of any
kind, he imprints on their minds a rule which is a
principle of action.

Now just as man, by such pronouncements, im-
presses a kind of inward principle of action on the
man that is subject to him, so God imprints on the
whole of nature the principles of its proper actions.
And so, in this way, God is said to command the
whole of nature, according to Ps. cxlviii. 6: *He hath
made a decree, and it shall not pass away.* And thus
all actions and movements of the whole of nature are
subject to the eternal law. Consequently irrational
creatures are subject to the eternal law, through
being moved by Divine providence; but not, as ra-

tional creatures are, through understanding the Divine commandment.

Reply Obj. 1. The impression of an inward active principle is to natural things, what the promulgation of law is to men: because law, by being promulgated, imprints on man a directive principle of human actions, as stated above.

Reply Obj. 2. Irrational creatures neither partake of nor are obedient to human reason: whereas they do partake of the Divine Reason by obeying it; because the power of Divine Reason extends over more things than human reason does. And as the members of the human body are moved at the command of reason, and yet do not partake of reason, since they have no apprehension subordinate to reason; so too irrational creatures are moved by God, without, on that account, being rational.

Reply Obj. 3. Although the defects which occur in natural things are outside the order of particular causes, they are not outside the order of universal causes, especially of the First Cause, *i.e.*, God, from Whose providence nothing can escape, as stated in the First Part (Q. XXII., A. 2). And since the eternal law is the type of Divine providence, as stated above (A. 1), hence the defects of natural things are subject to the eternal law.

Sixth Article

WHETHER ALL HUMAN AFFAIRS ARE SUBJECT TO THE ETERNAL LAW?

We proceed thus to the Sixth Article:—

Objection 1. It would seem that not all human affairs are subject to the eternal law. For the Apostle says (Gal. v. 18): *If you are led by the spirit you are not under the law.* But the righteous who are the sons of God by adoption, are led by the spirit of God, according to Rom. viii. 14: *Whosoever are led by the Spirit of God, they are the sons of God.* Therefore not all men are under the eternal law.

Obj. 2. Further, the Apostle says (Rom. viii. 7): *The prudence* (Vulg., *wisdom*) *of the flesh is an enemy to God: for it is not subject to the law of God.* But many are those in whom the prudence of the flesh dominates. Therefore all men are not subject to the eternal law which is the law of God.

Obj. 3. Further, Augustine says (*De Lib. Arb.* i. 6) that *the eternal law is that by which the wicked deserve misery, the good, a life of blessedness.* But those who are already blessed, and those who are already lost, are not in the state of merit. Therefore they are not under the eternal law.

On the contrary, Augustine says (*De Civ. Dei,* xix. 12): *Nothing evades the laws of the most high Creator and Governor, for by Him the peace of the universe is administered.*

I answer that, There are two ways in which a thing is subject to the eternal law, as explained above (A. 5): first, by partaking of the eternal law by way of knowledge; secondly, by way of action and passion, i.e., by partaking of the eternal law by way of an inward motive principle: and in this second way, irrational creatures are subject to the eternal law, as stated above (*ibid.*). But since the rational nature, together with that which it has in common with all creatures, has something proper to itself inasmuch as it is rational, consequently it is subject to the eternal law in both ways; because while each rational creature has some knowledge of the eternal law, as stated above (A. 2), it also has a natural inclination to that which is in harmony with the eternal law; for *we are naturally adapted to be the recipients of virtue* (*Ethic.* ii. 1).

Both ways, however, are imperfect, and to a certain extent destroyed, in the wicked; because in them the natural inclination to virtue is corrupted by vicious habits, and, moreover, the natural knowledge of good is darkened by passions and habits of sin. But in the good both ways are found more perfect: because in them, besides the natural knowledge of good, there is the added knowledge of faith and wisdom; and again, besides the natural inclination to good, there is the added interior motive of grace and virtue.

Accordingly, the good are perfectly subject to the eternal law, as always acting according to it: whereas the wicked are subject to the eternal law, imperfectly as to their actions, indeed, since both their knowledge of good, and their inclination thereto, are imperfect: but this imperfection on the part of action is supplied on the part of passion, in so far as they suffer what the eternal law decrees concerning them, according as they fail to act in harmony with that law. Hence Augustine says (*De Lib. Arb.* i. 15): *I esteem that the righteous act according to the eternal law;* and (*De Catech. Rud.* xviii.): *Out of the just misery of the souls which deserted him, God knew how to furnish the inferior parts of His creation with most suitable laws.*

Reply Obj. 1. This saying of the Apostle may be understood in two ways. First, so that a man is said to be under the law, through being pinned down thereby, against his will, as by a load. Hence, on the same passage a gloss says that *he is under the law, who refrains from evil deeds, through fear of the punishment threatened by the law, and not from love of virtue.* In this way the spiritual man is not under the law, because he fulfils the law willingly, through charity which is poured into his heart by the Holy Ghost. Secondly, it can be understood as meaning that the works of a man, who is led by the Holy Ghost, are the works of the Holy Ghost rather than his own. Therefore, since the Holy Ghost is not under the law, as neither is the Son, as stated above (A. 4 *ad* 2); it follows that such works, in so far as they are of the Holy Ghost, are not under the law. The Apostle witnesses to this when he says (2 Cor. iii. 17): *Where the Spirit of the Lord is, there is liberty.*

Reply Obj. 2. The prudence of the flesh cannot be

subject to the law of God as regards action; since it inclines to actions contrary to the Divine law: yet it is subject to the law of God, as regards passion; since it deserves to suffer punishment according to the law of Divine justice. Nevertheless in no man does the prudence of the flesh dominate so far as to destroy the whole good of his nature; and consequently there remains in man the inclination to act in accordance with the eternal law. For we have seen above (Q. LXXXV., A. 2) that sin does not destroy entirely the good of nature.

Reply Obj. 3. A thing is maintained in the end and moved towards the end by one and the same cause: thus gravity which makes a heavy body rest in the lower place is also the cause of its being moved thither. We therefore reply that as it is according to the eternal law that some deserve happiness, others unhappiness, so it is by the eternal law that some are maintained in a happy state, others in an unhappy state. Accordingly both the blessed and the damned are under the eternal law.

QUESTION 94

OF THE NATURAL LAW

(In Six Articles)

WE must now consider the natural law; concerning which there are six points of inquiry: (1) What is the natural law? (2) What are the precepts of the natural law? (3) Whether all acts of virtue are prescribed by the natural law? (4) Whether the natural law is the same in all? (5) Whether it is changeable? (6) Whether it can be abolished from the heart of man?

FIRST ARTICLE

WHETHER THE NATURAL LAW IS A HABIT?

We proceed thus to the First Article:—

Objection 1. It would seem that the natural law is a habit. Because, as the Philosopher says (*Ethic.* ii. 5), *there are three things in the soul, power, habit, and passion.* But the natural law is not one of the soul's powers: nor is it one of the passions; as we may see by going through them one by one. Therefore the natural law is a habit.

Obj. 2. Further, Basil says that the conscience or *synderesis is the law of our mind;* which can only apply to the natural law. But the *synderesis* is a habit, as was shown in the First Part (Q. LXXIX., A. 12). Therefore the natural law is a habit.

Obj. 3. Further, the natural law abides in man always, as will be shown further on (A. 6). But man's reason, which the law regards, does not always think about the natural law. Therefore the natural law is not an act, but a habit.

On the contrary, Augustine says (*De Bono Conjug.*

xxi) that *a habit is that whereby something is done when necessary.* But such is not the natural law: since it is in infants and in the damned who cannot act by it. Therefore the natural law is not a habit.

I answer that, A thing may be called a habit in two ways. First, properly and essentially: and thus the natural law is not a habit. For it has been stated above (Q. XC., A. 1 *ad* 2) that the natural law is something appointed by reason, just as a proposition is a work of reason. Now that which a man does is not the same as that whereby he does it: for he makes a becoming speech by the habit of grammar. Since then a habit is that by which we act, a law cannot be a habit properly and essentially.

Secondly, the term habit may be applied to that which we hold by a habit: thus faith may mean that which we hold by faith. And accordingly, since the precepts of the natural law are sometimes considered by reason actually, while sometimes they are in the reason only habitually, in this way the natural law may be called a habit. Thus, in speculative matters, the indemonstrable principles are not the habit itself whereby we hold those principles, but are the principles the habit of which we possess.

Reply Obj. 1. The Philosopher proposes there to discover the genus of virtue; and since it is evident that virtue is a principle of action, he mentions only those things which are principles of human acts, viz., powers, habits and passions. But there are other things in the soul besides these three: there are acts; thus *to will* is in the one that wills; again, things known are in the knower; moreover its own natural properties are in the soul, such as immortality and the like.

Reply Obj. 2. *Synderesis* is said to be the law of our mind, because it is a habit containing the precepts of the natural law, which are the first principles of human actions.

Reply Obj. 3. This argument proves that the natural law is held habitually: and this is granted.

To the argument advanced in the contrary sense we reply that sometimes a man is unable to make use of that which is in him habitually, on account of some impediment; thus, on account of sleep, a man is unable to use the habit of science. In like manner, through the deficiency of his age, a child cannot use the habit of understanding of principles, or the natural law, which is in him habitually.

SECOND ARTICLE

WHETHER THE NATURAL LAW CONTAINS SEVERAL PRECEPTS, OR ONE ONLY?

We proceed thus to the Second Article:—

Objection 1. It would seem that the natural law contains, not several precepts, but one only. For law is a kind of precept, as stated above (Q. XCII., A. 2). If therefore there were many precepts of the natural law, it would follow that there are also many natural laws.

Obj. 2. Further, the natural law is consequent to

human nature. But human nature, as a whole, is one; though, as to its parts, it is manifold. Therefore, either there is but one precept of the law of nature, on account of the unity of nature as a whole; or there are many, by reason of the number of parts of human nature. The result would be that even things relating to the inclination of the concupiscible faculty belong to the natural law.

Obj. 3. Further, law is something pertaining to reason, as stated above (Q. XC., A. 1). Now reason is but one in man. Therefore there is only one precept of the natural law.

On the contrary, The precepts of the natural law in man stand in relation to practical matters, as the first principles to matters of demonstration. But there are several first indemonstrable principles. Therefore there are also several precepts of the natural law.

I answer that, As stated above (Q. XCI., A. 3), the precepts of the natural law are to the practical reason, what the first principles of demonstrations are to the speculative reason; because both are self-evident principles. Now a thing is said to be self-evident in two ways: first, in itself; secondly, in relation to us. Any proposition is said to be self-evident in itself, if its predicate is contained in the notion of the subject: although, to one who knows not the definition of the subject, it happens that such a proposition is not self-evident. For instance, this proposition, *Man is a rational being,* is, in its very nature, self-evident, since who says *man,* says *a rational being:* and yet to one who knows not what a

man is, this proposition is not self-evident. Hence it
is that, as Boethius says (*De Hebdom.*), certain
axioms or propositions are universally self-evident to
all; and such are those propositions whose terms are
known to all, as, *Every whole is greater than its part*,
and, *Things equal to one and the same are equal to
one another*. But some propositions are self-evident
only to the wise, who understand the meaning of the
terms of such propositions: thus to one who under-
stands that an angel is not a body, it is self-evident
that an angel is not circumscriptively in a place: but
this is not evident to the unlearned, for they cannot
grasp it.

Now a certain order is to be found in those things
that are apprehended universally. For that which, before aught else, falls under apprehension, is *being,* the
notion of which is included in all things whatsoever
a man apprehends. Wherefore the first indemonstrable
principle is that *the same thing cannot be affirmed
and denied at the same time,* which is based on the
notion of *being* and *not-being:* and on this principle
all others are based, as is stated in *Metaph.* iv., text.
9. Now as *being* is the first thing that falls under
the apprehension simply, so *good* is the first thing
that falls under the apprehension of the practical
reason, which is directed to action: since every agent
acts for an end under the aspect of good. Consequently the first principle in the practical reason is
one founded on the notion of good, viz., that *good is
that which all things seek after*. Hence this is the
first precept of law, that *good is to be done and en-*

sued, and evil is to be avoided. All other precepts of
the natural law are based upon this: so that whatever
the practical reason naturally apprehends as man's
good (or evil) belongs to the precepts of the natural
law as something to be done or avoided.

Since, however, good has the nature of an end, and
evil, the nature of a contrary, hence it is that all
those things to which man has a natural inclination,
are naturally apprehended by reason as being good,
and consequently as objects of pursuit, and their con-
traries as evil, and objects of avoidance. Wherefore
according to the order of natural inclinations, is the
order of the precepts of the natural law. Because in
man there is first of all an inclination to good in accordance with the nature which he has in common
with all substances: inasmuch as every substance seeks
the preservation of its own being, according to its
nature: and by reason of this inclination, whatever
is a means of preserving human life, and of warding
off its obstacles, belongs to the natural law. Secondly,
there is in man an inclination to things that pertain to
him more specially, according to that nature which
he has in common with other animals: and in virtue
of this inclination, those things are said to belong to
the natural law, *which nature has taught to all animals,** such as sexual intercourse, education of off-
spring and so forth. Thirdly, there is in man an inclination to good, according to the nature of his reason, which nature is proper to him: thus man has a
natural inclination to know the truth about God, and

* *Pandect. Just.* I., tit. i.

to live in society: and in this respect, whatever pertains to this inclination belongs to the natural law; for instance, to shun ignorance, to avoid offending those among whom one has to live, and other such things regarding the above inclination.

Reply Obj. 1. All these precepts of the law of nature have the character of one natural law, inasmuch as they flow from one first precept.

Reply Obj. 2. All the inclinations of any parts whatsoever of human nature, *e.g.*, of the concupiscible and irascible parts, in so far as they are ruled by reason, belong to the natural law, and are reduced to one first precept, as stated above: so that the precepts of the natural law are many in themselves, but are based on one common foundation.

Reply Obj. 3. Although reason is one in itself, yet it directs all things regarding man; so that whatever can be ruled by reason, is contained under the law of reason.

Third Article

WHETHER ALL ACTS OF VIRTUE ARE PRESCRIBED BY THE NATURAL LAW?

We proceed thus to the Third Article:—

Objection 1. It would seem that not all acts of virtue are prescribed by the natural law. Because, as stated above (Q. XC., A. 2) it is essential to a law that it be ordained to the common good. But some acts of virtue are ordained to the private good of the individual, as is evident especially in regard to acts of temperance. Therefore not all acts of virtue are the subject of natural law.

Obj. 2. Further, every sin is opposed to some virtuous act. If therefore all acts of virtue are prescribed by the natural law, it seems to follow that all sins are against nature: whereas this applies to certain special sins.

Obj. 3. Further, those things which are according to nature are common to all. But acts of virtue are not common to all: since a thing is virtuous in one, and vicious in another. Therefore not all acts of virtue are prescribed by the natural law.

On the contrary, Damascene says (*De Fide Orthod.* iii. 4) that *virtues are natural.* Therefore virtuous acts also are a subject of the natural law.

I answer that, We may speak of virtuous acts in two ways: first, under the aspect of virtuous; secondly, as such and such acts considered in their proper species. If then we speak of acts of virtue, considered as virtuous, thus all virtuous acts belong to the natural law. For it has been stated (A. 2) that to the natural law belongs everything to which a man is inclined according to his nature. Now each thing is inclined naturally to an operation that is suitable to it according to its form: thus fire is inclined to give heat. Wherefore, since the rational soul is the proper form of man, there is in every man a natural inclination to act according to reason: and this is to act according to virtue. Consequently, considered thus, all acts of virtue are prescribed by the natural law: since each one's reason naturally dictates to him to act virtuously. But if we speak of virtuous acts, considered in themselves, i.e., in their proper species, thus not all virtuous acts are prescribed by the natural law: for many things are done virtuously, to which nature does not incline at first; but which, through the inquiry of reason, have been found by men to be conducive to well-living.

Reply Obj. 1. Temperance is about the natural concupiscenses of food, drink and sexual matters, which are indeed ordained to the natural common good, just as other matters of law are ordained to the moral common good.

Reply Obj. 2. By human nature we may mean either that which is proper to man—and in this sense all sins, as being against reason, are also against nature, as Damascene states (*De Fide Orthod*. ii. 30): or we may mean that nature which is common to man and other animals; and in this sense, certain special sins are said to be against nature; thus contrary to sexual intercourse, which is natural to all animals, is unisexual lust, which has received the special name of the unnatural crime.

Reply Obj. 3. This argument considers acts in themselves. For it is owing to the various conditions of men, that certain acts are virtuous for some, as being proportionate and becoming to them, while they are vicious for others, as being out of proportion to them.

FOURTH ARTICLE

WHETHER THE NATURAL LAW IS THE SAME IN ALL MEN?

We proceed thus to the Fourth Article:—

Objection 1. It would seem that the natural law is not the same in all. For it is stated in the Decretals (*Dist.* i.) that *the natural law is that which is contained in the Law and the Gospel*. But this is not common to all men; because, as it is written (Rom. x. 16), *all do not obey the gospel*. Therefore the natural law is not the same in all men.

Obj. 2. Further, *Things which are according to the law are said to be just*, as stated in *Ethic.* v. But it is stated in the same book that nothing is so universally just as not to be subject to change in regard to some men. Therefore even the natural law is not the same in all men.

Obj. 3. Further, as stated above (AA. 2, 3), to the natural law belongs everything to which a man is inclined according to his nature. Now different men are naturally inclined to different things; some to the desire of pleasures, others to the desire of honours, and other men to other things. Therefore there is not one natural law for all.

On the contrary, Isidore says (*Etym.* v. 4): *The natural law is common to all nations.*

I answer that, As stated above (AA. 2, 3), to the

natural law belongs those things to which a man is inclined naturally: and among these it is proper to man to be inclined to act according to reason. Now the process of reason is from the common to the proper, as stated in *Phys.* i. The speculative reason, however, is differently situated in this matter, from the practical reason. For, since the speculative reason is busied chiefly with necessary things, which cannot be otherwise than they are, its proper conclusions, like the universal principles, contain the truth without fail. The practical reason, on the other hand, is busied with contingent matters, about which human actions are concerned: and consequently, although there is necessity in the general principles, the more we descend to matters of detail, the more frequently we encounter defects. Accordingly then in speculative matters truth is the same in all men, both as to principles and as to conclusions: although the truth is not known to all as regards the conclusions, but only as regards the principles which are called common notions. But in matters of action, truth or practical rectitude is not the same for all, as to matters of detail, but only as to the general principles: and where there is the same rectitude in matters of detail, it is not equally known to all.

It is therefore evident that, as regards the general principles whether of speculative or of practical reason, truth or rectitude is the same for all, and is equally known by all. As to the proper conclusions of the speculative reason, the truth is the same for all, but is not equally known to all: thus it is true for all that the three angles of a triangle are together equal to two right angles, although it is not known to all. But as to the proper conclusions of the practical reason, neither is the truth or rectitude the same for all, nor, where it is the same, is it equally known by all. Thus it is right and true for all to act according to reason: and from this principle it follows as a proper conclusion, that goods entrusted to another should be restored to their owner. Now this is true for the majority of cases: but it may happen in a particular case that it would be injurious, and therefore unreasonable, to restore goods held in trust; for instance if they are claimed for the purpose of fighting against one's country. And this principle will be found to fail the more, according as we descend further into detail, *e.g.*, if one were to say that goods held in trust should be restored with such and such a guarantee, or in such and such a way; because the greater the number of conditions added, the greater the number of ways in which the principle may fail, so that it be not right to restore or not to restore.

Consequently we must say that the natural law, as to general principles, is the same for all, both as to rectitude and as to knowledge. But as to certain matters of detail, which are conclusions, as it were, of those general principles, it is the same for all in the majority of cases, both as to rectitude and as to knowledge; and yet in some few cases it may fail, both as to rectitude, by reason of certain obstacles (just as natures subject to generation and corruption fail in some few cases on account of some obstacle), and as to knowledge, since in some the reason is perverted by passion, or evil habit, or an evil disposition of nature; thus formerly, theft, although it is expressly contrary to the natural law, was not considered wrong among the Germans, as Julius Caesar relates (*De Bello Gall*. vi.).

Reply Obj. 1. The meaning of the sentence quoted is not that whatever is contained in the Law and the Gospel belongs to the natural law, since they contain many things that are above nature; but that whatever belongs to the natural law is fully contained in them. Wherefore Gratian, after saying that *the natural law is what is contained in the Law and the Gospel*, adds at once, by way of example, *by which everyone is commanded to do to others as he would be done by*.

Reply Obj. 2. The saying of the Philosopher is to be understood of things that are naturally just, not as general principles, but as conclusions drawn from them, having rectitude in the majority of cases, but failing in a few.

Reply Obj. 3. As, in man, reason rules and commands the other powers, so all the natural inclinations belonging to the other powers must needs be directed according to reason. Wherefore it is universally right for all men, that all their inclinations should be directed according to reason.

FIFTH ARTICLE

WHETHER THE NATURAL LAW CAN BE CHANGED?

We proceed thus to the Fifth Article:—

Objection 1. It would seem that the natural law can be changed. Because on Ecclus. xvii. 9, *He gave them instructions, and the law of life,* the gloss says: *He wished the law of the letter to be written, in order to correct the law of nature.* But that which is corrected is changed. Therefore the natural law can be changed.

Obj. 2. Further, the slaying of the innocent, adultery, and theft are against the natural law. But we find these things changed by God: as when God commanded Abraham to slay his innocent son (Gen. xxii. 2); and when He ordered the Jews to borrow and purloin the vessels of the Egyptians (Exod. xii. 35); and when He commanded Osee to take to himself *a wife of fornications* (Osee i. 2). Therefore the natural law can be changed.

Obj. 3. Further, Isidore says (*Etym.* v. 4) that *the possession of all things in common, and universal freedom, are matters of natural law.* But these things are seen to be changed by human laws. Therefore it seems that the natural law is subject to change.

On the contrary, It is said in the Decretals (*Dist.* v.): *The natural law dates from the creation of the rational creature. It does not vary according to time, but remains unchangeable.*

I answer that, A change in the natural law may be understood in two ways. First, by way of addition. In this sense nothing hinders the natural law from being changed: since many things for the benefit of human life have been added over and above the natural law, both by the Divine law and by human laws.

Secondly, a change in the natural law may be understood by way of subtraction, so that what previously was according to the natural law, ceases to be so. In this sense, the natural law is altogether unchangeable in its first principles: but in its secondary principles, which, as we have said (A. 4), are certain detailed proximate conclusions drawn from the first principles, the natural law is not changed so that what it prescribes be not right in most cases. But it may be changed in some particular cases of rare occurrence, through some special causes hindering the observance of such precepts, as stated above (A. 4).

Reply Obj. 1. The written law is said to be given for the correction of the natural law, either because it supplies what was wanting to the natural law; or because the natural law was perverted in the hearts of some men, as to certain matters, so that they esteemed those things good which are naturally evil; which perversion stood in need of correction.

Reply Obj. 2. All men alike, both guilty and innocent, die the death of nature: which death of nature is inflicted by the power of God on account of original sin, according to 1 Kings ii. 6: *The Lord killeth and maketh alive.* Consequently, by the command of God, death can be inflicted on any man, guilty or innocent, without any injustice whatever.— In like manner adultery is intercourse with another's wife; who is allotted to him by the law emanating from God. Consequently intercourse with any woman, by the command of God, is neither adultery nor fornication.—The same applies to theft, which is the taking of another's property. For whatever is taken by the command of God, to Whom all things belong, is not taken against the will of its owner, whereas it is in this that theft consists.—Nor is it only in human things, that whatever is commanded by God is right; but also in natural things, whatever is done by God, is, in some way, natural, as stated in the First Part (Q. CV., A. 6 *ad* 1).

Reply Obj. 3. A thing is said to belong to the natural law in two ways. First, because nature inclines thereto: *e.g.,* that one should not do harm to another. Secondly, because nature did not bring in the contrary: thus we might say that for man to be naked is of the natural law, because nature did not give him clothes, but art invented them. In this sense, *the possession of all things in common and universal freedom* are said to be of the natural law, because, to wit, the distinction of possessions and slavery were not brought in by nature, but devised by human reason for the benefit of human life. Accordingly the law of nature was not changed in this respect, except by addition.

SIXTH ARTICLE

WHETHER THE LAW OF NATURE CAN BE ABOLISHED FROM THE HEART OF MAN?

We proceed thus to the Sixth Article:—

Objection 1. It would seem that the natural law can be abolished from the heart of man. Because on Rom. ii. 14, *When the Gentiles who have not the law*, etc., a gloss says that *the law of righteousness, which sin had blotted out, is graven on the heart of man when he is restored by grace*. But the law of righteousness is the law of nature. Therefore the law of nature can be blotted out.

Obj. 2. Further, the law of grace is more efficacious than the law of nature. But the law of grace is blotted out by sin. Much more therefore can the law of nature be blotted out.

Obj. 3. Further, that which is established by law is made just. But many things are enacted by men, which are contrary to the law of nature. Therefore the law of nature can be abolished from the heart of man.

On the contrary, Augustine says (*Conf.* ii.): *Thy law is written in the hearts of men, which iniquity itself effaces not*. But the law which is written in men's hearts is the natural law. Therefore the natural law cannot be blotted out.

I answer that, As stated above (AA. 4, 5), there

belong to the natural law, first, certain most general precepts, that are known to all; and secondly, certain secondary and more detailed precepts, which are, as it were, conclusions following closely from first principles. As to those general principles, the natural law, in the abstract, can nowise be blotted out from men's hearts. But it is blotted out in the case of a particular action, in so far as reason is hindered from applying the general principle to a particular point of practice, on account of concupiscence or some other passion, as stated above (Q. LXXVII., A. 2).—But as to the other, *i.e.*, the secondary precepts, the natural law can be blotted out from the human heart, either by evil persuasions, just as in speculative matters errors occur in respect of necessary conclusions; or by vicious customs and corrupt habits, as among some men, theft, and even unnatural vices, as the Apostle states (Rom. i.), were not esteemed sinful.

Reply Obj. 1. Sin blots out the law of nature in particular cases, not universally, except perchance in regard to the secondary precepts of the natural law, in the way stated above.

Reply Obj. 2. Although grace is more efficacious than nature, yet nature is more essential to man, and therefore more enduring.

Reply Obj. 3. This argument is true of the secondary precepts of the natural law, against which some legislators have framed certain enactments which are unjust.

QUESTION 95

OF HUMAN LAW

(*In Four Articles*)

WE must now consider human law; and (1) this law considered in itself; (2) its power; (3) its mutability. Under the first head there are four points of inquiry: (1) Its utility. (2) Its origin (3) Its quality. (4) Its division.

FIRST ARTICLE

WHETHER IT WAS USEFUL FOR LAWS TO BE FRAMED BY MEN?

We proceed thus to the First Article:—

Objection 1. It would seem that it was not useful for laws to be framed by men. Because the purpose of every law is that man be made good thereby, as stated above (Q. XCII., A. 1). But men are more to be induced to be good willingly by means of admonitions, than against their will, by means of laws. Therefore there was no need to frame laws.

Obj. 2. Further, as the Philosopher says (*Ethic.* v. 4), *men have recourse to a judge as to animate justice.* But animate justice is better than inanimate justice, which is contained in laws. Therefore it would have been better for the execution of justice to be entrusted to the decision of judges, than to frame laws in addition.

Obj. 3. Further, every law is framed for the direction of human actions, as is evident from what has been stated above (Q. XC., AA. 1, 2). But since human actions are about singulars, which are infinite in number, matters pertaining to the direction of human actions cannot be taken into sufficient consideration except by a wise man, who looks into each one of them. Therefore it would have been better for human acts to be directed by the judgment of wise men, than by the framing of laws. Therefore there was no need of human laws.

On the contrary, Isidore says (*Etym.* v. 20): *Laws were made that in fear thereof human audacity might be held in check, that innocence might be safeguarded in the midst of wickedness, and that the dread of punishment might prevent the wicked from doing harm.* But these things are most necessary to mankind. Therefore it was necessary that human laws should be made.

I answer that, As stated above (Q. LXIII., A. 1; Q. XCIV., A. 3), man has a natural aptitude for virtue; but the perfection of virtue must be acquired by man by means of some kind of training. Thus we observe that man is helped by industry in his necessities, for instance, in food and clothing. Certain

beginnings of these he has from nature, viz., his reason and his hands; but he has not the full compli-
ment, as other animals have, to whom nature has
given sufficiency of clothing and food. Now it is
difficult to see how man could suffice for himself in
the matter of this training: since the perfection of
virtue consists chiefly in withdrawing man from un-
due pleasures, to which above all man is inclined,
and especially the young, who are more capable of
being trained. Consequently a man needs to receive
this training from another, whereby to arrive at the
perfection of virtue. And as to those young people
who are inclined to acts of virtue, by their good
natural disposition, or by custom, or rather by the
gift of God, paternal training suffices, which is by
admonitions. But since some are found to be depraved,
and prone to vice, and not easily amenable to words,
it was necessary for such to be restrained from evil
by force and fear, in order that, at least, they might
desist from evildoing, and leave others in peace, and
that they themselves, by being habituated in this
way, might be brought to do willingly what hitherto
they did from fear, and thus become virtuous. Now
this kind of training, which compels through fear
of punishment, is the discipline of laws. Therefore,
in order that man might have peace and virtue, it
was necessary for laws to be framed: for, as the
Philosopher says (*Polit.* i. 2), *as man is the most
noble of animals, if he be perfect in virtue, so is he
the lowest of all, if he be severed from law and right-*

eousness; because man can use his reason to devise means of satisfying his lusts and evil passions, which other animals are unable to do.

Reply Obj. 1. Men who are well disposed are led willingly to virtue by being admonished better than by coercion: but men who are evilly disposed are not led to virtue unless they are compelled.

Reply Obj. 2. As the Philosopher says (*Rhet.* i. 1), *it is better that all things be regulated by law, than left to be decided by judges:* and this for three reasons. First, because it is easier to find a few wise men competent to frame right laws, than to find the many who would be necessary to judge aright of each single case.—Secondly, because those who make laws consider long beforehand what laws to make; whereas judgment on each single case has to be pronounced as soon as it arises: and it is easier for man to see what is right, by taking many instances into consideration, than by considering one solitary fact. —Thirdly, because lawgivers judge in the abstract and of future events; whereas those who sit in judgment judge of things present, towards which they are affected by love, hatred, or some kind of cupidity; wherefore their judgment is perverted.

Since then the animated justice of the judge is not found in every man, and since it can be deflected, it was necessary, whenever possible, for the law to determine how to judge, and for very few matters to be left to the decision of men.

Reply Obj. 3. Certain individual facts which cannot be covered by the law *have necessarily to be committed to judges,* as the Philosopher says in the same passage: for instance, *concerning something that has happened or not happened,* and the like.

WHETHER EVERY HUMAN LAW IS DERIVED FROM
THE NATURAL LAW?

We proceed thus to the Second Article:—

Objection 1. It would seem that not every human law is derived from the natural law. For the Philosopher says (*Ethic.* v. 7) that *the legal just is that which originally was a matter of indifference.* But those things which arise from the natural law are not matters of indifference. Therefore the enactments of human laws are not all derived from the natural law.

Obj. 2. Further, positive law is contrasted with natural law, as stated by Isidore (*Etym.* v. 4) and the Philosopher (*Ethic.* v., *loc. cit.*). But those things which flow as conclusions from the general principles of the natural law belong to the natural law, as stated above (Q. XCIV., A. 4). Therefore that which is established by human law does not belong to the natural law.

Obj. 3. Further, the law of nature is the same for all; since the Philosopher says (*Ethic.* v. 7) that *the natural just is that which is equally valid everywhere.* If therefore human laws were derived from the natural laws, it would follow that they too are the same for all: which is clearly false.

Obj. 4. Further, it is possible to give a reason for things which are derived from the natural law. But *it is not possible to give the reason for all the legal enactments of the lawgivers,* as the jurist says.* Therefore not all human laws are derived from the natural law.

On the contrary, Tully says (*Rhetor.* ii.): *Things which emanated from nature and were approved by custom, were sanctioned by fear and reverence for the laws.*

I answer that, As Augustine says (*De Lib. Arb.* i. 5), *that which is not just seems to be no law at all:* wherefore the force of a law depends on the extent of its justice. Now in human affairs a thing is said to be just, from being right, according to the rule of reason. But the first rule of reason is the law of nature, as is clear from what has been stated above (Q. XCI., A. 2 *ad* 2). Consequently every human law has just so much of the nature of law, as it is derived from the law of nature. But if in any point it deflects from the law of nature, it is no longer a law but a perversion of law.

But it must be noted that something may be derived from the natural law in two ways: first, as a conclusion from premises, secondly, by way of determination of certain generalities. The first way is like to that by which, in sciences, demonstrated conclusions are drawn from the principles: while the

* *Pandect. Justin.* lib. i. ff., tit. iii., art. v., *De Leg. et Senat.*

second mode is likened to that whereby, in the arts, general forms are particularized as to details: thus the craftsman needs to determine the general form of a house to some particular shape. Some things are therefore derived from the general principles of the natural law, by way of conclusions; *e.g.*, that *one must not kill* may be derived as a conclusion from the principle that *one should do harm to no man*: while some are derived therefrom by way of determination; *e.g.*, the law of nature has it that the evildoer should be punished; but that he be punished in this or that way, is a determination of the law of nature.

Accordingly both modes of derivation are found in the human law. But those things which are derived in the first way, are contained in human law not as emanating therefrom exclusively, but have some force from the natural law also. But those things which are derived in the second way, have no other force than that of human law.

Reply Obj. 1. The Philosopher is speaking of those enactments which are by way of determination or specification of the precepts of the natural law.

Reply Obj. 2. This argument avails for those things that are derived from the natural law, by way of conclusions.

Reply Obj. 3. The general principles of the natural law cannot be applied to all men in the same way on account of the great variety of human affairs: and hence arises the diversity of positive laws among various people.

Reply Obj. 4. These words of the Jurist are to b‿ understood as referring to decisions of rulers in determining particular points of the natural law: on which determinations the judgment of expert and prudent men is based as on its principles; in so far, to wit, as they see at once what is the best thing to decide.

Hence the Philosopher says (*Ethic.* vi. 11) that in such matters, *we ought to pay as much attention to the undemonstrated sayings and opinions of persons who surpass us in experience, age and prudence, as to their demonstrations.*

Third Article

WHETHER ISIDORE'S DESCRIPTION OF THE QUALITY OF POSITIVE LAW IS APPROPRIATE?

We proceed thus to the Third Article:—

Objection 1. It would seem that Isidore's description of the quality of positive law is not appropriate, when he says (*Etym.* v. 21): *Law shall be virtuous, just, possible to nature, according to the custom of the country, suitable to place and time, necessary, useful; clearly expressed, lest by its obscurity it lead to misunderstanding; framed for no private benefit, but for the common good.* Because he had previously expressed the quality of law in three conditions, saying that *law is anything founded on reason, provided that it foster religion, be helpful to discipline, and*

further the common weal. Therefore it was needless
to add any further conditions to these.

Obj. 2. Further, Justice is included in honesty, as
Tully says (*De Offic.* vii.). Therefore after saying
honest it was superfluous to add *just.*

Obj. 3. Further, written law is condivided with
custom, according to Isidore (*Etym.* ii. 10). Therefore it should not be stated in the definition of law
that it is *according to the custom of the country.*

Obj. 4. Further, a thing may be necessary in two
ways. It may be necessary simply, because it cannot
be otherwise: and that which is necessary in this way,
is not subject to human judgment, wherefore human
law is not concerned with necessity of this kind.
Again a thing may be necessary for an end: and this
necessity is the same as usefulness. Therefore it is
superfluous to say both *necessary* and *useful.*

On the contrary stands the authority of Isidore.

I answer that, Whenever a thing is for an end, its
form must be determined proportionately to that
end; as the form of a saw is such as to be suitable
for cutting (*Phys.* ii., text. 88). Again, everything
that is ruled and measured must have a form proportionate to its rule and measure. Now both these
conditions are verified of human law: since it is both
something ordained to an end; and is a rule or measure ruled or measured by a higher measure. And this
higher measure is twofold, viz., the Divine law and
the natural law, as explained above (A. 2; Q. XCIII.,
A. 3). Now the end of human law is to be useful to
man, as the Jurist states.* Wherefore Isidore in de-

* *Pandect. Just. lib.* xxv. ff., tit. iii., *De Leg. et Senat.*

termining the nature of law, lays down, at first, three conditions; viz., that it *foster religion,* inasmuch as it is proportionate to the Divine law; that it be *helpful to discipline,* inasmuch as it is proportionate to the natural law; and that it *further the common weal,* inasmuch as it is proportionate to the utility of mankind.

All the other conditions mentioned by him are reduced to these three. For it is called virtuous because it fosters religion. And when he goes on to say that it should be *just, possible to nature, according to the customs of the country, adapted to place and time,* he implies that it should be helpful to discipline. For human discipline depends first on the order of reason, to which he refers by saying *just:*—secondly, it depends on the ability of the agent; because discipline should be adapted to each one according to his ability, taking also into account the ability of nature (for the same burdens should be not laid on children as on adults); and should be according to human customs; since man cannot live alone in society, paying no heed to others:—thirdly, it depends on certain circumstances, in respect of which he says, *adapted to place and time.*—The remaining words, *necessary, useful, etc.,* mean that law should further the common weal: so that *necessity* refers to the removal of evils; *usefulness* to the attainment of good; *clearness of expression,* to the need of preventing any harm ensuing from the law itself.—And since, as stated above (Q. XC., A. 2), law is ordained

to the common good, this is expressed in the last part
of the description.

This suffices for the Replies to the Objections.

FOURTH ARTICLE

WHETHER ISIDORE'S DIVISION OF HUMAN LAWS IS APPROPRIATE?

We proceed thus to the Fourth Article:—

Objection 1. It would seem that Isidore wrongly
divided human statutes or human law (*Etym.* v. 4
seqq.). For under this law he includes the *law of nations,* so called, because, as he says, *nearly all nations use
it.* But as he says, *natural law is that which is common
to all nations.* Therefore the law of nations is not contained under positive human law, but rather under
natural law.

Obj. 2. Further, those laws which have the same
force, seem to differ not formally but only materially.
But *statutes, decrees of the commonalty, senatorial
decrees,* and the like which he mentions (*ibid.,* 9),
all have the same force. Therefore they do not differ,
except materially. But art takes no notice of such a
distinction: since it may go on to infinity. Therefore
this division of human laws is not appropriate.

Obj. 3. Further, just as, in the state, there are
princes, priests and soldiers, so are there other human
offices. Therefore it seems that, as this division includes *military law,* and *public law,* referring to

priests and magistrates; so also it should include other laws pertaining to other offices of the state.

Obj. 4. Further, those things that are accidental should be passed over. But it is accidental to law that it be framed by this or that man. Therefore it is unreasonable to divide laws according to the names of lawgivers, so that one be called the *Cornelian* law, another the *Falcidian* law, etc.

On the contrary, The authority of Isidore (Obj. 1) suffices.

I answer that, A thing can of itself be divided in respect of something contained in the notion of that thing. Thus a soul either rational or irrational is contained in the notion of animal: and therefore animal is divided properly and of itself in respect of its being rational or irrational; but not in the point of its being white or black, which are entirely beside the notion of animal. Now, in the notion of human law, many things are contained, in respect of any of which human law can be divided properly and of itself. For in the first place it belongs to the notion of human law, to be derived from the law of nature, as explained above (A. 2). In this respect positive law is divided into the *law of nations* and *civil law,* according to the two ways in which something may be derived from the law of nature, as stated above (A. 2). Because, to the law of nations belong those things which are derived from the law of nature, as conclusions from premises, *e.g.,* just buyings and sellings, and the like, without which men cannot live together, which is a point of the law of nature, since man is by nature a social animal, as is proved in *Polit.* i. 2. But those things which are derived from the law of nature by way of particular determination, belong to the civil law, according as each state decides on what is best for itself.

Secondly, it belongs to the notion of human law, to be ordained to the common good of the state. In this respect human law may be divided according to the different kinds of men who work in a special way for the common good: *e.g.*, priests, by praying to God for the people; princes, by governing the people; soldiers, by fighting for the safety of the people. Wherefore certain special kinds of law are adapted to these men.

Thirdly, it belongs to the notion of human law, to be framed by that one who governs the community of the state, as shown above (Q. XC., A. 3). In this respect, there are various human laws according to the various forms of government. Of these, according to the Philosopher (*Polit.* iii. 10) one is *monarchy*, i.e., when the state is governed by one; and then we have *Royal Ordinances*. Another form is *aristocracy*, i.e., government by the best men or men of highest rank; and then we have the *Authoritative legal opinions* (*Responsa Prudentum*) and *Decrees of the Senate* (*Senatus consulta*). Another form is *oligarchy*, i.e., government by a few rich and powerful men; and then we have *Praetorian*, also called *Honorary*, law. Another form of government is that of the people, which is called democracy, and there we have *Decrees of the commonalty* (*Plebiscita*). There is also tyrannical government, which is altogether corrupt, which, therefore, has no corresponding law. Finally, there is a form of government made up of all these, and which is the best: and in this respect we have *law sanctioned by the Lords and Commons*, as stated by Isidore (*loc. cit.*).

Fourthly, it belongs to the notion of human law to direct human actions. In this respect, according to the various matters of which the law treats, there are various kinds of laws, which are sometimes named after their authors: thus we have the *Lex Julia* about adultery, the *Lex Cornelia* concerning assasins, and so on, differentiated in this way, not on account of the authors, but on account of the matters to which they refer.

Reply Obj. 1. The law of nations is indeed, in some way, natural to man, in so far as he is a reasonable being, because it is derived from the natural law by way of a conclusion that is not very remote from its premisses. Wherefore men easily agreed thereto. Nevertheless it is distinct from the natural law, especially from that natural law which is common to all animals.

The Replies to the other Objections are evident from what has been said.

QUESTION 96

OF THE POWER OF HUMAN LAW

(*In Six Articles*)

WE must now consider the power of human law. Under this head there are six points of inquiry: (1) Whether human law should be framed for the community? (2) Whether human law should repress all vices? (3) Whether human law is competent to direct all acts of virtue? (4) Whether it binds man in conscience? (5) Whether all men are subject to human law? (6) Whether those who are under the law may act beside the letter of the law?

FIRST ARTICLE

WHETHER HUMAN LAW SHOULD BE FRAMED FOR THE COMMUNITY RATHER THAN FOR THE INDIVIDUAL?

We proceed thus to the First Article:—

Objection 1. It would seem that human law should be framed not for the community, but rather for the individual. For the Philosopher says (*Ethic*. v. 7) that *the legal just . . . includes all particular acts of legislation . . . and all those matters which are the subject of decrees,* which are also individual matters, since decrees are framed about individual actions. Therefore law is framed not only for the community, but also for the individual.

Obj. 2. Further, law is the director of human acts, as stated above (Q. XC., AA. 1, 2). But human acts are about individual matters. Therefore human laws should be framed, not for the community, but rather for the individual.

Obj. 3. Further, law is a rule and measure of human acts, as stated above (Q. XC., AA. 1, 2). But a measure should be most certain, as stated in *Metaph.* x. Since therefore in human acts no general proposition can be so certain as not to fail in some individual cases, it seems that laws should be framed not in general but for individual cases.

On the contrary, The jurist says (*Pandect. Justin,* lib. i., tit. iii., art. ii., *De legibus,* etc.) that *laws should be made to suit the majority of instances; and they are not framed according to what may possibly happen in an individual case.*

I answer that, Whatever is for an end should be proportionate to that end. Now the end of law is the common good; because, as Isidore says (*Etym.* v. 21) that *law should be framed, not for any private benefit, but for the common good of all the citizens.* Hence human laws should be proportionate to the common good. Now the common good comprises many things. Wherefore laws should take account of many things, as to persons, as to matters, and as to times. Because the community of the state is composed of many persons; and its good is procured by

many actions; nor is it established to endure for only
a short time, but to last for all time by the citizens
succeeding one another, as Augustine says (*De Civ.
Dei* ii. 21; xxii. 6).

Reply Obj. 1. The Philosopher (*Ethic. v.* 7) divides
the legal just, i.e., positive law, into three parts. For
some things are laid down simply in a general way:
and these are the general laws. Of these he says that *the
legal is that which originally was a matter of indifference, but which, when enacted, is so no longer:* as the
fixing of the ransom of a captive.—Some things affect
the community in one respect, and individuals in another. These are called *privileges,* i.e., *private laws,* as
it were, because they regard private persons, although
their power extends to many matters; and in regard
to these, he adds, *and further, all particular acts of
legislation.*—Other matters are legal, not through being laws, but through being applications of general
laws to particular cases: such are decrees which have
the force of law; and in regard to these, he adds *all
matters subject to decrees.*

Reply Obj. 2. A principle of direction should be
applicable to many; wherefore (*Metaph.* x., text. 4)
the Philosopher says that all things belonging to one
genus, are measured by one, which is the principle in
that genus. For if there were as many rules or measures as there are things measured or ruled, they would
cease to be of use, since their use consists in being
applicable to many things. Hence law would be of no
use, if it did not extend further than to one single
act. Because the decrees of prudent men are made for

the purpose of directing individual actions; whereas law is a general precept, as stated above (Q. XCII., A. 2, Obj. 2).

Reply Obj. 3. *We must not seek the same degree of certainty in all things (Ethic. i. 3).* Consequently in contingent matters, such as natural and human things, it is enough for a thing to be certain, as being true in the greater number of instances, though at times and less frequently it fail.

SECOND ARTICLE

WHETHER IT BELONGS TO HUMAN LAW TO REPRESS ALL VICES?

We proceed thus to the Second Article:—

Objection 1. It would seem that it belongs to human law to repress all vices. For Isidore says (*Etym.* v. 20) that *laws were made in order that, in fear thereof, man's audacity might be held in check.* But it would not be held in check sufficiently, unless all evils were repressed by law. Therefore human law should repress all evils.

Obj. 2. Further, the intention of the lawgiver is to make the citizens virtuous. But a man cannot be virtuous unless he forbear from all kinds of vice. Therefore it belongs to human law to repress all vices.

Obj. 3. Further, human law is derived from the natural law, as stated above (Q. XCV., A. 2). But all vices are contrary to the law of nature. Therefore human law should repress all vices.

On the contrary, We read in *De Lib. Arb.* i. 5: *It seems to me that the law which is written for the governing of the people rightly permits these things, and that Divine providence punishes them.* But Divine providence punishes nothing but vices. Therefore human law rightly allows some vices, by not repressing them.

I answer that, As stated above (Q. XC., AA. 1, 2), law is framed as a rule or measure of human acts. Now a measure should be homogeneous with that which it measures, as stated in *Metaph.* x., text. 3, 4, since different things are measured by different measures. Wherefore laws imposed on men should also be in keeping with their condition, for, as Isidore says (*Etym.* v. 21), law should be *possible both according to nature, and according to the customs of the country.* Now possibility or faculty of action is due to an interior habit or disposition: since the same thing is not possible to one who has not a virtuous habit, as is possible to one who has. Thus the same is not possible to a child as to a full-grown man: for which reason the law for children is not the same as for adults, since many things are permitted to children, which in an adult are punished by law or at any rate are open to blame. In like manner many things are permissible to men not perfect in virtue, which would be intolerable in a virtuous man.

Now human law is framed for a number of human beings, the majority of whom are not perfect in virtue. Wherefore human laws do not forbid all vices, from which the virtuous abstain, but only the more grievous vices, from which it is possible for the majority to abstain; and chiefly those that are to the hurt of others, without the prohibition of which human society could not be maintained: thus human law prohibits murder, theft and suchlike.

Reply Obj. 1. Audacity seems to refer to the assailing of others. Consequently it belongs to those sins chiefly whereby one's neighbour is injured: and these sins are forbidden by human law, as stated.

Reply Obj. 2. The purpose of human law is to lead men to virtue, not suddenly, but gradually. Wherefore it does not lay upon the multitude of imperfect men the burdens of those who are already virtuous, viz., that they should abstain from all evil. Otherwise these imperfect ones, being unable to bear such precepts, would break out into yet greater evils: thus it is written (Prov. xxx. 33): *He that violently bloweth his nose, bringeth out blood;* and (Matth. ix. 17) that if *new wine,* i.e., precepts of a perfect life, is *put into old bottles,* i.e., into imperfect men, *the bottles break, and the wine runneth out,* i.e., the precepts are despised, and those men, from contempt, break out into evils worse still.

Reply Obj. 3. The natural law is a participation in us of the eternal law: while human law falls short of the eternal law. Now Augustine says (*De Lib. Arb.* i. 5): *The law which is framed for the government of states, allows and leaves unpunished many things that are punished by Divine providence. Nor,*

*if this law does not attempt to do everything, is this
a reason why it should be blamed for what it does.*
Wherefore, too, human law does not prohibit everything that is forbidden by the natural law.

THIRD ARTICLE

WHETHER HUMAN LAW PRESCRIBES ACTS OF ALL THE VIRTUES?

We proceed thus to the Third Article:—
Objection 1. It would seem that human law does
not prescribe acts of all the virtues. For vicious acts
are contrary to acts of virtue. But human law does
not prohibit all vices, as stated above (A. 2). Therefore neither does it prescribe all acts of virtue.

Obj. 2. Further, a virtuous act proceeds from a
virtue. But virtue is the end of law; so that whatever
is from a virtue, cannot come under a precept of law.
Therefore human law does not prescribe all acts of
virtue.

Obj. 3. Further, law is ordained to the common
good, as stated above (Q. XC., A. 2). But some acts
of virtue are ordained, not to the common good, but
to private good. Therefore the law does not prescribe
all acts of virtue.

On the contrary, The Philosopher says (*Ethic.* v.
1) that the law *prescribes the performance of the
acts of a brave man, . . . and the acts of the temperate
man, . . . and the acts of the meek man: and in like*

manner as regards the other virtues and vices, pre-scribing the former, forbidding the latter.

I answer that, The species of virtues are distin-guished by their objects, as explained above (Q. LIV., A. 2; Q. LX., A. 1; Q. LXII., A. 2). Now all the objects of virtues can be referred either to the private good of an individual, or to the common good of the multitude: thus matters of fortitude may be achieved either for the safety of the state, or for upholding the rights of a friend, and in like manner with the other virtues. But law, as stated above (Q. XC., A. 2) is ordained to the common good. Wherefore there is no virtue whose acts cannot be prescribed by the law. Nevertheless human law does not prescribe con-cerning all the acts of every virtue: but only in re-gard to those that are ordainable to the common good, —either immediately, as when certain things are done directly for the common good,—or mediately, as when a lawgiver prescribes certain things pertaining to good order, whereby the citizens are directed in the upholding of the common good of justice and peace.

Reply Obj. 1. Human law does not forbid all vicious acts, by the obligation of a precept, as neither does it prescribe all acts of virtue. But it forbids certain acts of each vice, just as it prescribes some acts of each virtue.

Reply Obj. 2. An act is said to be an act of virtue in two ways. First, from the fact that a man does something virtuous; thus the act of justice is to do what is right, and an act of fortitude is to do brave things: and in this way law prescribes certain acts of virtue.—Secondly an act of virtue is when a man does a virtuous thing in a way in which a virtuous man does it. Such an act always proceeds from virtue: and it does not come under a precept of law, but is the end at which every lawgiver aims.

Reply Obj. 3. There is no virtue whose act is not ordainable to the common good, as stated above, either mediately or immediately.

Fourth Article

WHETHER HUMAN LAW BINDS A MAN IN CONSCIENCE?

We proceed thus to the Fourth Article:—

Objection 1. It would seem that human law does not bind a man in conscience. For an inferior power has no jurisdiction in a court of higher power. But the power of a man, which frames human law, is beneath the Divine power. Therefore human law cannot impose its precept in a Divine court, such as is the court of conscience.

Obj. 2. Further, the judgment of conscience depends chiefly on the commandments of God. But sometimes God's commandments are made void by human laws, according to Matth. xv. 6: *You have made void the commandment of God for your tradition.* Therefore human law does not bind a man in conscience.

Obj. 3. Further, human laws often bring loss of

character and injury on man, according to Isa. x. 1 et seq.: *Woe to them that make wicked laws, and when they write, write injustice; to oppress the poor in judgment, and do violence to the cause of the humble of My people.* But it is lawful for anyone to avoid oppression and violence. Therefore human laws do not bind man in conscience.

On the contrary, It is written (1 Pet. ii. 19): *This is thanksworthy, if for conscience . . . a man endure sorrows, suffering wrongfully.*

I answer that, Laws framed by man are either just or unjust. If they be just, they have the power of binding in conscience, from the eternal law whence they are derived, according to Prov. viii. 15: *By Me kings reign, and lawgivers decree just things.* Now laws are said to be just, both from the end, when, to wit, they are ordained to the common good,—and from their author, that is to say, when the law that is made does not exceed the power of the lawgiver,— and from their form, when, to wit, burdens are laid on the subjects, according to an equality of proportion and with a view to the common good. For, since one man is a part of the community, each man, in all that he is and has, belongs to the community; just as a part, in all that it is, belongs to the whole; wherefore nature inflicts a loss on the part, in order to save the whole: so that on this account, such laws as these, which impose proportionate burdens, are just and binding in conscience, and are legal laws.

On the other hand laws may be unjust in two ways: first, by being contrary to human good, through being opposed to the things mentioned above:—either in respect of the end, as when an authority imposes on his subjects burdensome laws, conducive, not to the common good, but rather to his own cupidity or vainglory;—or in respect of the author, as when a man makes a law that goes beyond the power committed to him;—or in respect of the form, as when burdens are imposed unequally on the community, although with a view to the common good. The like are acts of violence rather than laws; because as Augustine says (*De Lib. Arb.* i. 5), *a law that is not just, seems to be no law at all.* Wherefore such laws do not bind in conscience, except perhaps in order to avoid scandal or disturbance, for which cause a man should even yield his right, according to Matth. v. 40, 41: *If a man . . . take away thy coat, let go thy cloak also unto him; and whosoever will force thee one mile, go with him other two.*

Secondly, laws may be unjust through being opposed to the Divine good: such are the laws of tyrants inducing to idolatry, or to anything else contrary to the Divine law: and laws of this kind must nowise be observed, because, as stated in Acts v. 29, *we ought to obey God rather than men.*

Reply Obj. 1. As the Apostle says (Rom. xiii. 1, 2), all human power is from God . . . *therefore he that resisteth the power,* in matters that are within its scope, *resisteth the ordinance of God;* so that he becomes guilty according to his conscience.

Reply Obj. 2. This argument is true of laws that are contrary to the commandments of God, which is beyond the scope of (human) power. Wherefore in such matters human law should not be obeyed.

Reply Obj. 3. This argument is true of a law that inflicts unjust hurt on its subjects. The power that man holds from God does not extend to this: wherefore neither in such matters is man bound to obey the law, provided he avoid giving scandal or inflicting a more grievous hurt.

FIFTH ARTICLE

WHETHER ALL ARE SUBJECT TO THE LAW?

We proceed thus to the Fifth Article:—

Objection 1. It would seem that not all are subject to the law. For those alone are subject to a law for whom a law is made. But the Apostle says (1 Tim. i. 9): *The law is not made for the just man.* Therefore the just are not subject to the law.

Obj. 2. Further, Pope Urban says:* *He that is guided by a private law need not for any reason be bound by the public law.* Now all spiritual men are led by the private law of the Holy Ghost, for they are the sons of God, of whom it is said (Rom. viii. 14): *Whosoever are led by the Spirit of God, they are the sons of God.* Therefore not all men are subject to human law.

* *Decret.* caus. xix., qu. 2.

Obj. 3. Further, the jurist says* that *the sovereign is exempt from the laws.* But he that is exempt from the law is not bound thereby. Therefore not all are subject to the law.

On the contrary, The Apostle says (Rom. xiii. 1): *Let every soul be subject to the higher powers.* But *subjection* to a power seems to imply subjection to the laws framed by that power. Therefore all men should be subject to human law.

I answer that, As stated above (Q. XC., AA. 1, 2; A. 3 *ad* 2), the notion of law contains two things; first, that it is a rule of human acts; secondly, that it has coercive power. Wherefore a man may be subject to law in two ways. First, as the regulated is subject to the regulator: and, in this way, whoever is subject to a power, is subject to the law framed by that power. But it may happen in two ways that one is not subject to a power. In one way, by being altogether free from its authority: hence the subjects of one city or kingdom are not bound by the laws of the sovereign of another city or kingdom, since they are not subject to his authority. In another way, by being under a yet higher law; thus the subject of a proconsul should be ruled by his command, but not in those matters in which the subject receives his orders from the emperor: for in these matters, he is not bound by the mandate of the lower authority, since he is directed by that of a higher. In this way, one who is simply subject to a law, may not be sub-

---

* *Pandect. Justin.* i. ff., tit. 3, *De Leg. et Senat.*

ject thereto in certain matters, in respect of which he is ruled by a higher law.

Secondly, a man is said to be subject to a law as the coerced is subject to the coercer. In this way the virtuous and righteous are not subject to the law, but only the wicked. Because coercion and violence are contrary to the will: but the will of the good is in harmony with the law, whereas the will of the wicked is discordant from it. Wherefore in this sense the good are not subject to the law, but only the wicked.

Reply Obj. 1. This argument is true of subjection by way of coercion: for, in this way, *the law is not made for the just men:* because *they are a law to themselves,* since they *shew the work of the law written in their hearts,* as the Apostle says (Rom. ii. 14, 15). Consequently the law does not enforce itself upon them as it does on the wicked.

Reply Obj. 2. The law of the Holy Ghost is above all law framed by man: and therefore spiritual men, in so far as they are led by the law of the Holy Ghost, are not subject to the law in those matters that are inconsistent with the guidance of the Holy Ghost. Nevertheless the very fact that spiritual men are subject to law, is due to the leading of the Holy Ghost, according to 1 Pet. ii. 13: *Be ye subject . . . to every human creature for God's sake.*

Reply Obj. 3. The sovereign is said to be *exempt from the law,* as to its coercive power; since, properly speaking, no man is coerced by himself, and law has no coercive power save from the authority of the sovereign. Thus then is the sovereign said to be exempt from the law, because none is competent to pass sentence on him, if he acts against the law. Wherefore on Ps. L. 6: *To Thee only have I sinned*, a gloss says that *there is no man who can judge the deeds of a king*.—But as to the directive force of law, the sovereign is subject to the law by his own will, according to the statement (*Extra, De Constit.* cap. *Cum omnes*) that *whatever law a man makes for another, he should keep himself. And a wise authority* says: 'Obey the law that thou makest thyself.'* Moreover the Lord reproaches those who *say and do not;* and who *bind heavy burdens and lay them on men's shoulders, but with a finger of their own they will not move them* (Matth. xxiii. 3, 4). Hence, in the judgment of God, the sovereign is not exempt from the law, as to its directive force; but he should fulfil it of his own free-will and not of constraint.— Again the sovereign is above the law, in so far as, when it is expedient, he can change the law, and dispense in it according to time and place.

SIXTH ARTICLE

WHETHER HE WHO IS UNDER A LAW MAY ACT BESIDE THE LETTER OF THE LAW?

We proceed thus to the Sixth Article:—

Objection 1. It seems that he who is subject to a law may not act beside the letter of the law. For

---

* Dionysius Cato, *Dist. de Moribus.*

Augustine says (*De Vera Relig.* xxxi): *Although men judge about temporal laws when they make them, yet when once they are made they must pass judgment not on them, but according to them.* But if anyone disregard the letter of the law, saying that he observes the intention of the lawgiver, he seems to pass judgment on the law. Therefore it is not right for one who is under a law to disregard the letter of the law, in order to observe the intention of the lawgiver.

Obj. 2. Further, he alone is competent to interpret the law who can make the law. But those who are subject to the law cannot make the law. Therefore they have no right to interpret the intention of the lawgiver, but should always act according to the letter of the law.

Obj. 3. Further, every wise man knows how to explain his intention by words. But those who framed the laws should be reckoned wise: for Wisdom says (Prov. viii. 15): *By Me kings reign, and lawgivers decree just things.* Therefore we should not judge of the intention of the lawgiver otherwise than by the words of the law.

On the contrary, Hilary says (*De Trin.* iv.): *The meaning of what is said is according to the motive for saying it: because things are not subject to speech, but speech to things.* Therefore we should take account of the motive of the lawgiver, rather than of his very words.

I answer that, As stated above (A. 4), every law is directed to the common weal of men, and derives the force and nature of law accordingly. Hence the jurist says:* *By no reason of law, or favour of equity, is it allowable for us to interpret harshly, and render burdensome, those useful measures which have been enacted for the welfare of man.* Now it happens often that the observance of some point of law conduces to the common weal in the majority of instances, and yet, in some cases, is very hurtful. Since then the lawgiver cannot have in view every single case, he shapes the law according to what happens most frequently, by directing his attention to the common good. Wherefore if a case arise wherein the observance of that law would be hurtful to the general welfare, it should not be observed. For instance, suppose that in a beseiged city it be an established law that the gates of the city are to be kept closed, this is good for public welfare as a general rule: but, if it were to happen that the enemy are in pursuit of certain citizens, who are defenders of the city, it would be a great loss to the city, if the gates were not opened to them: and so in that case the gates ought to be opened, contrary to the letter of the law, in order to maintain the common weal, which the lawgiver had in view.

Nevertheless it must be noted, that if the observance of the law according to the letter does not involve any sudden risk needing instant remedy, it is not competent for everyone to expound what is useful and what is not useful to the state: those alone can do this who are in authority, and who, on account

* *Pandect. Justin.* lib. i. ff., tit. 3, *De Leg. et Senat.*

of suchlike cases, have the power to dispense from the laws. If, however, the peril be so sudden as not to allow of the delay involved by referring the matter to authority, the mere necessity brings with it a dispensation, since necessity knows no law.

Reply Obj. 1. He who in case of necessity acts beside the letter of the law, does not judge of the law; but of a particular case in which he sees that the letter of the law is not to be observed.

Reply Obj. 2. He who follows the intention of the lawgiver, does not interpret the law simply; but in a case in which it is evident, by reason of the manifest harm, that the lawgiver intended otherwise. For if it be a matter of doubt, he must either act according to the letter of the law, or consult those in power.

Reply Obj. 3. No man is so wise as to be able to take account of every single case; wherefore he is not able sufficiently to express in words all those things that are suitable for the end he has in view. And even if a lawgiver were able to take all the cases into consideration, he ought not to mention them all, in order to avoid confusion: but should frame the law according to that which is of most common occurrence.

QUESTION 97

OF CHANGE IN LAWS

(*In Four Articles*)

WE must now consider change in laws: under which head there are four points of inquiry: (1) Whether human law is changeable? (2) Whether it should be always changed, whenever anything better occurs? (3) Whether it is abolished by custom, and whether custom obtains the force of law? (4) Whether the application of human law should be changed by dispensation of those in authority?

FIRST ARTICLE

WHETHER HUMAN LAW SHOULD BE CHANGED IN ANY WAY?

We proceed thus to the First Article:—

Objection 1. It would seem that human law should not be changed in any way at all. Because human law is derived from the natural law, as stated above (Q. XCV., A. 2). But the natural law endures unchangeably. Therefore human law should also remain without any change.

Obj. 2. Further, as the Philosopher says (*Ethic.* v.

5), a measure should be absolutely stable. But human law is the measure of human acts, as stated above (Q. XC., AA. 1, 2). Therefore it should remain without change.

Obj. 3. Further, it is of the essence of law to be just and right, as stated above (Q. XCV., A. 2). But that which is right once is right always. Therefore that which is law once, should be always law.

On the contrary, Augustine says (*De Lib. Arb.* i. 6): *A temporal law, however just, may be justly changed in course of time.*

I answer that, As stated above (Q. XCI., A. 3), human law is a dictate of reason, whereby human acts are directed. Thus there may be two causes for the just change of human law: one on the part of reason; the other on the part of man whose acts are regulated by law. The cause on the part of reason is that it seems natural to human reason to advance gradually from the imperfect to the perfect. Hence, in speculative sciences, we see that the teaching of the early philosophers was imperfect, and that it was afterwards perfected by those who succeeded them. So also in practical matters: for those who first endeavoured to discover something useful for the human community, not being able by themselves to take everything into consideration, set up certain institutions which were deficient in many ways; and these were changed by subsequent lawgivers who made institutions that might prove less frequently deficient in respect of the common weal.

On the part of man, whose acts are regulated by

law, the law can be rightly changed on account of
the changed condition of man, to whom different
things are expedient according to the difference of his
condition. An example is proposed by Augustine (*De
Lib. Arb. i. 6*): *If the people have a sense of modera-
tion and responsibility, and are most careful guardians
of the common weal, it is right to enact a law allowing such a people to choose their own magistrates for
the government of the commonwealth. But if, as time
goes on, the same people become so corrupt as to sell
their votes, and entrust the government to scoundrels
and criminals; then the right of appointing their
public officials is rightly forfeit to such a people, and
the choice devolves to a few good men.*

Reply obj. 1. The natural law is a participation of
the eternal law, as stated above (Q. XCI., A. 2), and
therefore endures without change, owing to the un-
changeableness and perfection of the Divine Reason,
the Author of nature. But the reason of man is
changeable and imperfect: wherefore his law is subject to change.—Moreover the natural law contains
certain universal precepts, which are everlasting:
whereas human law contains certain particular precepts, according to various emergencies.

Reply Obj. 2. A measure should be as enduring as
possible. But nothing can be absolutely unchangeable
in things that are subject to change. And therefore
human law cannot be altogether unchangeable.

Reply Obj. 3. In corporal things, right is predicated
absolutely: and therefore, as far as itself is concerned,
always remains right. But right is predicated of law

with reference to the common weal, to which one and the same thing is not always adapted, as stated above: wherefore rectitude of this kind is subject to change.

SECOND ARTICLE

WHETHER HUMAN LAW SHOULD ALWAYS BE CHANGED, WHENEVER SOMETHING BETTER OCCURS?

We proceed thus to the Second Article:—

Objection 1. It would seem that human law should be changed, whenever something better occurs. Because human laws are devised by human reason, like other arts. But in the other arts, the tenets of former times give place to others, if something better occurs. Therefore the same should apply to human laws.

Obj. 2. Further, by taking note of the past we can provide for the future. Now unless human laws had been changed when it was found possible to improve them, considerable inconvenience would have ensued; because the laws of old were crude in many points. Therefore it seems that laws should be changed, whenever anything better occurs to be enacted.

Obj. 3. Further, human laws are enacted about single acts of man. But we cannot acquire perfect knowledge in singular matters, except by experience, which *requires time,* as stated in *Ethic.* ii. Therefore it seems

that as time goes on it is possible for something better
to occur for legislation.

On the contrary, It is stated in the Decretals (*Dist.*
xii. 5): *It is absurd, and a detestable shame, that we
should suffer those traditions to be changed which we
have received from the fathers of old.*

I answer that, As stated above (A. 1), human law
is rightly changed, in so far as such change is conducive to the common weal. But, to a certain extent,
the mere change of law is of itself prejudicial to the
common good: because custom avails much for the
observance of laws, seeing that what is done contrary
to general custom, even in slight matters, is looked
upon as grave. Consequently, when a law is changed,
the binding power of the law is diminished, in so far
as custom is abolished. Wherefore human law should
never be changed, unless, in some way or other, the
common weal be compensated according to the extent
of the harm done in this respect. Such compensation
may arise either from some very great and very evident benefit conferred by the new enactment; or
from the extreme urgency of the case, due to the fact
that either the existing law is clearly unjust, or its
observance extremely harmful. Wherefore the jurist
says* that *in establishing new laws, there should be
evidence of the benefit to be derived, before departing
from a law which has long been considered just.*

Reply Obj. 1. Rules of art derive their force from
reason alone: and therefore whenever something better

* *Pandect. Justin.* lib. i. ff., tit. 4, *De Constit. Princip.*

occurs, the rule followed hitherto should be changed. But *laws derive very great force from custom,* as the Philosopher states (*Polit.* ii. 5): consequently they should not be quickly changed.

Reply Obj. 2. This argument proves that laws ought to be changed: not in view of any improvement, but for the sake of a great benefit or in a case of great urgency, as stated above. This answer applies also to the Third Objection.

Third Article

WHETHER CUSTOM CAN OBTAIN FORCE OF LAW?

We proceed thus to the Third Article:—

Objection 1. It would seem that custom cannot obtain force of law, nor abolish a law. Because human law is derived from the natural law and from the Divine law, as stated above (Q. XCIII., A. 3; Q. XCV., A. 2). But human custom cannot change either the law of nature or the Divine law. Therefore neither can it change human law.

Obj. 2. Further, many evils cannot make one good. But he who first acted against the law, did evil. Therefore by multiplying such acts, nothing good is the result. Now a law is something good; since it is a rule of human acts. Therefore law is not abolished by custom, so that the mere custom should obtain force of law.

Obj. 3. Further, the framing of laws belongs to those public men whose business it is to govern the community; wherefore private individuals cannot make laws. But custom grows by the acts of private individuals. Therefore custom cannot obtain force of law, so as to abolish the law.

On the contrary, Augustine says (*Ep. ad Casulan,* xxxvi.): *The customs of God's people and the institutions of our ancestors are to be considered as laws. And those who throw contempt on the customs of the Church ought to be punished as those who disobey the law of God.*

I answer that, All law proceeds from the reason and will of the lawgiver; the Divine and natural laws from the reasonable will of God; the human law from the will of man, regulated by reason. Now just as human reason and will, in practical matters, may be made manifest by speech, so may they be made known by deeds: since seemingly a man chooses as good that which he carries into execution. But it is evident that by human speech, law can be both changed and expounded, in so far as it manifests the interior movement and thought of human reason. Wherefore by actions also, especially if they be repeated, so as to make a custom, law can be changed and expounded; and also something can be established which obtains force of law, in so far as by repeated external actions, the inward movement of the will, and concepts of reason are most effectually declared; for when a thing is done again and again, it seems to proceed from a deliberate judgment of reason. Accordingly, custom has the force of a law, abolishes law, and is the interpreter of law.

Reply Obj. 1. The natural and Divine laws proceed from the Divine will, as stated above. Wherefore they cannot be changed by a custom proceeding from the will of man, but only by Divine authority. Hence it is that no custom can prevail over the Divine or natural laws: for Isidore says (*Synon.* ii. 16). *Let custom yield to authority: evil customs should be eradicated by law and reason.*

Reply Obj. 2. As stated above (Q. XCVI., A. 6), human laws fail in some cases: wherefore it is possible sometimes to act beside the law; namely, in a case where the law fails; yet the act will not be evil. And when such cases are multiplied, by reason of some change in man, then custom shows that the law is no longer useful: just as it might be declared by the verbal promulgation of a law to the contrary. If, however, the same reason remains, for which the law was useful hitherto, then it is not the custom that prevails against the law, but the law that overcomes the custom: unless perhaps the sole reason for the law seeming useless, be that it is not *possible according to the custom of the country,** which has been stated to be one of the conditions of law. For it is not easy to set aside the custom of a whole people.

Reply Obj. 3. The people among whom a custom is introduced may be of two conditions. For if they are free, and able to make their own laws, the consent

* *Cf.* Q. XCV., A. 3.

of the whole people expressed by a custom counts far more in favour of a particular observance, than does the authority of the sovereign, who has not the power to frame laws, except as representing the people. Wherefore although each individual cannot make laws, yet the whole people can. If however the people have not the free power to make their own laws, or to abolish a law made by a higher authority; nevertheless with such a people a prevailing custom obtains force of law, in so far as it is tolerated by those to whom it belongs to make laws for that people: because by the very fact that they tolerate it they seem to approve of that which is introduced by custom.

FOURTH ARTICLE

WHETHER THE RULERS OF THE PEOPLE CAN DISPENSE FROM HUMAN LAWS?

We proceed thus to the Fourth Article:—

Objection 1. It would seem that the rulers of the people cannot dispense from human laws. For the law is established for the *common weal,* as Isidore says (*Etym.* v. 21). But the common good should not be set aside for the private convenience of an individual: because, as the Philosopher says (*Ethic.* i. 2), *the good of the nation is more godlike than the good of one man.* Therefore it seems that a man should not be dispensed from acting in compliance with the general law.

Obj. 2. Further, those who are placed over others are commanded as follows (Deut. i. 17): *You shall hear the little as well as the great; neither shall you respect any man's person, because it is the judgment of God.* But to allow one man to do that which is equally forbidden to all, seems to be respect of persons. Therefore the rulers of a community cannot grant such dispensations, since this is against a precept of the Divine law.

Obj. 3. Further, human law, in order to be just, should accord with the natural and Divine laws: else it would not *foster religion,* nor be *helpful to discipline,* which is requisite to the nature of law, as laid down by Isidore (*Etym.* v. 3). But no man can dispense from the Divine and natural laws. Neither, therefore, can he dispense from the human law.

On the contrary, The Apostle says (1 Cor. ix. 17): *A dispensation is committed to me.*

I answer that, Dispensation, properly speaking, denotes a measuring out to individuals of some common goods: thus the head of a household is called a dispenser, because to each member of the household he distributes work and necessaries of life in due weight and measure. Accordingly in every community a man is said to dispense, from the very fact that he directs how some general precept is to be fulfilled by each individual. Now it happens at times that a precept, which is conducive to the common weal as a general rule, is not good for a particular individual, or in some particular case, either because it would hinder some greater good, or because it would be the occasion of some evil, as explained above (Q. XCVI., A. 6). But it would be dangerous to leave this to the discretion of each individual, except perhaps by reason of an evident and sudden emergency, as stated above (*ibid.*). Consequently he who is placed over a community is empowered to dispense in a human law that rests upon his authority, so that, when the law fails in its application to persons or circumstances, he may allow the precept of the law not to be observed. If however he grant this permission without any such reason, and of his mere will, he will be an unfaithful or an imprudent dispenser: unfaithful, if he has not the common good in view; imprudent, if he ignores the reasons for granting dispensations. Hence Our Lord says (Luke xii. 42): *Who, thinkest thou, is the faithful and wise dispenser* (Douay,—*steward*), whom *his lord setteth over his family?*

Reply Obj. 1. When a person is dispensed from observing the general law, this should not be done to the prejudice of, but with the intention of benefiting, the common good.

Reply Obj. 2. It is not respect of persons if unequal measures are served out to those who are themselves unequal. Wherefore when the condition of any person requires that he should reasonably receive special treatment, it is not respect of persons if he be the object of special favour.

Reply Obj. 3. Natural law, so far as it contains general precepts, which never fail, does not allow of dispensation. In the other precepts, however, which are as conclusions of the general precepts, man sometimes grants a dispensation: for instance, that a loan should not be paid back to the betrayer of his country, or something similar. But to the Divine law each man stands as a private person to the public law to which he is subject. Wherefore just as none can dispense from public human law, except the man from whom the law derives its authority, or his delegate; so, in the precepts of the Divine law, which are from God, none can dispense but God, or the man to whom He may give special power for that purpose.